THE MAGIC OF THE SOUL

Applying Spiritual Power to Daily Living

PATRICK J. HARBULA

PEAK PUBLICATIONS

Published by
Peak Publications
2593 Young Avenue
Thousand Oaks, CA 91360
805-241-4832

Publisher's Cataloging-in-Publication Data
Harbula, Patrick J.
    The magic of the soul : applying spiritual power to daily living / Patrick
J. Harbula. -- 1st ed.
    p. cm.
    Includes bibliographical references and index.
    LCCN 2002106186
    ISBN 0-9715565-0-4

    1. Spiritual life.   I. Title.

BL624.H37 2003   291.4
                              QBI02-200403

Cover Design: Ravi Balasuriya
Editing: Kim Robinson
Proofreading: Kathryn Journey and Tracy Marcynzsyn

Contents

Guided Exercises

Acknowledgments

Thanks to all those who have helped me on my path to the magic of my soul including but not limited to Father Harris, Frank Boyle, Hanz Ram, Willie Ram, Cathy Harbula, Amy Jackson, Mrs. Nash, David Madeck, Richard Scharch, Kevin Kiley, Sue Edwards, Mark Bashara, Jason Celich, Howard Shatski, Lori Salsbury, Carl Earn, Sheila Winston, Serena Souza, Stephanie Souza, Joy Bernhart, Arnold Bernhart, Jenilee Barnum, Patricia Hartswick, Ruby Bergner, Rosa Junod, Karen Clark, Elizabeth Robinson-Barnum, Alan Braun, Betty White, Ida Sims, Lee Perry, Michwel Heril, David Ramsdale, Raymond Powers, Naomi Snyder, Liz Winstead, Jessica Migdall, Corey Leland, Sharlene Szymusiak, Ruth Clark, Ken Lasorella, Linda Stern, Mike Findley, Sandra Oster, Stephen Fiske, Pearl Dorris, Fumi Johns, Phil Estrada, Tom Purdy, Sharon O'Laughlin, David Ginsburg, David Cole, Marilyn Barry, Shakura, Stewart Wilde, Bruce Finn, Patty Finn, Megan Finn, Jeremy Finn, David Mark, Barbara Mark, CJ Boyle, John-Alexis Viereck, Alverna Taylor, Glenda Christian, Martin Herril, Jeriel Smith, Jerry Ann Smith, Tom Carney, Mary Carney, Meg Bundeck, Sun Wolf, Feline Butcher, Philip Taylor, Scott Hooper, Kristin Nelson, Ani Ayvazian, Gillian Dickens, John Shaw, Lisa Cuevas, Ravi Balasuriya, David McCune, Blaise Simqu, Larry Harpel, Bob Lesoine, Kent Neff, Jeff Burman, David Howard, Leticia Rodriguez, Jane Watson, Joy Dial, Cheryl Neuenkirk, Roger Palmer, Scott Larson, Inabelle Gallette, Jane Watson, Beverly Gaard, Dana St. Claire, Maria Villeda, Ana-Maria Baca, Dennis Merritt Jones, Maureen Hoyt, Bob Luckin, Judith Churchman, Carrie Lauer, Susan Curtis, John Lennon, Roger Waters, Oprah Winfrey, Roberto Assagioli, Molidoma Somé, Pir Valayat Khan, Mathew Fox, Swami Satchidananda, Ram Dass, David Spangler, Howard Zitko, Marilyn Ferguson, Mother Teresa, Mahatma Ghandi, Socrates, Plato, Descartes, Jesus Christ, Sai Baba, Djwhal Khul, Buddha, Lao Tsu, and especially Eleanor Harbula,

Warren Harbula, Chris Boyle, Rick Bednarec, Tricia Harbula, Elmer Hammersmith, Rosetta Hammersmith, Earl Barnum, Vivian King, Ed Porrazzo, Karen Orell, Kim Robinson, Jonathan Enderica, Elizabeth Warren, Alison Warren, Corina Villeda, and my magical Angels.

Extended thanks to the professionals who helped me to complete this book: Kim Robinson for her expert editing and guidance. Ravi Balasuriya for his exquisite cover design, Bob Lesoine for the beautiful music that graces the guided meditations, Richard Blair for expert audio mixing, Jason Love and Barbara Mark for additional editing, Kathryn Journey and Tracy Marcynzsyn for excellent proofreading, and Eleanor Harbula, Raymond Powers, Jonathan Enderica, David Mark, Mary Harpel, Curstin Apperle, and Jenilee Barnum for their wonderful content feedback.

Foreword

Teachers, saints, prophets, and sages have written about and described the oneness of all life throughout time. Now more than ever, increasing numbers of people are bringing these ancient concepts down to the level of daily experience. When we are able to walk beyond the doorway of our personal identification, we step into a world that is alive with love, splendor, creative power, and profound interconnectedness. We can honor ourselves for our wonderful uniqueness and at the same time recognize and experience ourselves as part of a spiritual dynamic that is present in everyone and everything. The magic of the soul is a practice to help open the door and offer guidance along the path into this world of magical opportunity.

The word magic implies something mystical or supernatural. This practice of which I write can indeed lead us into mystical realms, but it is important to recognize that it is a natural process. The extraordinary is only unique when it is a rare occurrence. As more and more people step into the magic of their souls through this or other spiritual practices, magical and miraculous states of being become more and more commonplace. This magic is not that of a slight-of-hand artist or of some macabre practice, but the magic of true spiritual alchemy. I speak of the magic that is written about by poets, spiritual teachers, and sages throughout history who have experienced or at least enjoyed a glimpse of the power lying beneath our ordinary experience. This is the world of interconnectedness, of oneness with all, of unconditional love and unlimited possibilities.

This book was written not only to inspire the *idea* of our interconnectedness and our power, but the *experience* of it. In some places you are asked to stop and experience the ideas presented. The centered phrases are meant to encourage deeper thought and reflection. Imagine that these messages are the voice of your own soul speaking to you, encouraging you to pause and receive its wisdom, peace, and magical capabilities. Try rewording them as "I" statements and use them as affirmations. There may be more methods and techniques to access soul magic than you can absorb and integrate during the period of time you are reading this book. Use those that speak to your heart and set the others aside for another time.

I recommend reading this book more than once and revisiting the areas to which you relate most. Many of the meditative exercises are presented on *The Magic of the Soul* audio CD accompanying the book. Experiencing the exercises will deepen your understanding of the concepts presented. Use the exercises on a regular basis that inspire you to deeper levels of understanding your own path, your own soul expression. Modify them and make them part of your ongoing practice.

We live at an exciting time in the history of our planet when information pointing to spiritual awareness has reached a peak. Why are the philosophies that have previously been reserved for esoteric and mystical circles now so available and accepted by larger numbers of people? Because we have never been more ready to receive and integrate them. Many of us are ready to step forward into our true roles as co-creators with the Divine Creative Principle, ready to create the magic of our souls. My sincere hope is that in reading and practicing the information in this book, your experience will be as enjoyable and magical as the writing of it has been for me. It is our divine heritage to live a life of fulfillment and joyful service, to experience the magic of life, the magic of the soul.

In this fourth printing, I have made a few minor changes and additions. Many of the exercises printed in the book that are not on the accompanying audio CD are now available in audio format at http://www.livingpurposeinstitute.com/meditation.htm. I have also included a new term that I have given to the practice of looking for the magic in every experience, which is "radical gratitude." I expanded *Meditation on Symbols* and the *Arrow Exercise*.

I hope to meet you at one of my many appearances (a calendar of which you can view at the new website as well), so I can experience firsthand, the magic of you!

Introduction

My spiritual journey was transformed when I was twenty years old after an intense period of meditation that lasted a couple of months. I had been practicing meditation for about two years and had been a philosophical thinker all of my life. But at that time, I did not have any definite spiritual belief. I knew there must be some kind of Higher Power, but I had long since let go of the concept of God that I had learned as a child. One evening, following a deep meditation, I had an experience that others have termed cosmic consciousness and what to me was direct contact with my soul and with God or the Divine Creative Principle that pervades all existence. For a period of about an hour, I experienced what I can only describe as being one with the Infinite Universe. I asked questions and received answers that could not possibly have come from my own mind. This experience changed my view of spiritual reality forever. I could clearly see that the entire universe works in perfect harmony as one eternal, symbiotic organism. Every energetic cell affects every other cell and every thought of every being affects every other being. The law of cause and effect, or karma, is a living, breathing dynamic. And everything occurs at the same moment. There is no sense of time or space in this state of supreme reality.

I understood from that moment of cosmic consciousness—a moment that has never been duplicated in my life but that I approach in meditation each day—that we are all one. My purpose in life became to empower others to a deeper understanding of themselves and to help people experience our essential oneness. My purpose has evolved through many different arenas in my adult life, including tennis instructor, minister, writer, cofounder and executive editor of *Meditation* magazine (a national consumer magazine published from 1985 to 1992), and most recently as a director for Sage Publications, a world-renowned, social science publisher. All of my successes, both personally and in empowering others, have been a result of applying the principles set forth in this book. I have learned how to apply these principles both through failure and success, struggle and surrender.

I recognize the spiritual truth at the heart of all religious systems, but I do not belong to any one specific faith. I consider myself a member and supporter of all paths of spiritual growth and worship. I find the variety of customs and rituals of different religious and philosophical systems richly beautiful and refreshing. I also recognize that the deeper one goes into one's own faith, the more unified becomes the understanding of Spirit. As a great spiritual teacher once said to me, "There are many roads home."

The impetus for writing this book is born from my heart's desire to share the profound joy and fulfillment I have gained from practicing The Magic of the Soul. My intent is to offer an experience of soul to the reader—a map that can guide those interested enough to follow it into its splendor—to a life of increased magic, wonder, fulfillment, peace, and creative service. Thank you for allowing me to walk with you for a while as you explore the magic of your soul.

1

Spiritual Magic

A young man was exploring a cave near his home one day when the beam from his flashlight ignited a faint sparkle on the ground. He instantly flashed the light back to the spot, walked over, and began surveying the cavern floor. Again the sparkle appeared. He leaned down and picked up the source of the reflection and found a fairly ordinary looking rock. As he studied it more closely, he realized it was a raw diamond. He buffed it and discovered that it had to be six or seven carats large. He was not an expert, but he knew it would be worth a handsome price if it were of decent quality. He placed the jewel in his pocket and explored the floor for more jewels. He searched deep into the cave but found no other evidence of anything of value.

When he left the cave, he reached back into his pocket to find only a large hole, as though the diamond had burned through the material. He immediately raced back into the cave and hurriedly retraced his steps, scouring the ground for his briefly owned prize. He searched for hours into the night but to no avail. He returned the following day and the day after that.

He soon lost his job as a carpenter because he failed to show up for work as a result of searching for the diamond that he knew would land him a fortune. Why waste time on a job, when he would be wealthy once he found his treasure, the one that was rightfully his? He eventually lost his home as he ran out of money to pay rent. He set up a tent near the cave so he could spend more time searching each day. He became a hermit, letting go of all relationships and hobbies to focus on his obsessive quest.

Twenty years passed in the blink of an eye. He finally realized he had wasted at least a quarter of his life on something that may not have been as valuable as he had imagined. He decided that he would spend one more day searching, and if he did not find the diamond, he would give up and start a normal life. He searched and searched on hands and knees until they were both stained with sooty blood. He worked for eighteen hours straight knowing this would be his last chance. Now he wanted to find the diamond as much to appease his guilt over wasting his life as to enjoy the illusive fortune he had originally sought.

Exhausted beyond all means, he fell onto his back in despair. It hit him how ridiculous he must have looked lying there on the floor, dirty, exhausted, and completely without a life. He began laughing at the shear absurdity of his folly. He could not stop laughing as his mind flooded with realizations that could only come from letting go of a twenty-year-long obsession. Realizations about everything he had missed out on: the pride of contributing to the world through his craft, the joy of sharing in relationships and raising a family, the love of friends. In that moment, he found his jewel. He recognized that had he not spent those twenty years searching, he might not ever have appreciated as much as he did in that moment the value of a simple, meaningful life. He felt grateful for his lesson and vowed to enjoy life for each moment from that day on.

The moral of this story is quite evident and represents what we humans often do even if not to such a mythical extreme. We tend to look outside ourselves for answers and to the future for happiness. You probably thought our friend was going to find the diamond once he gave up, but he did not find that physical object. He found something much more valuable in his heart—a jewel of understanding.

But there is one final part of the story I haven't mentioned yet. As he lay on his back laughing for hours, his flashlight glazed across the walls of the cave and eventually revealed to him a ceiling dripping with raw diamonds. In looking down for twenty years for his single diamond, he missed the fact that he was surrounded by a much greater reward—a magical array of beautiful treasures beyond anything he could imagine. What is surrounding you that you may be missing by paying attention to the mundane or the limitations that you have learned to accept? What might you stumble upon if you surrender to a higher principle of life?

Open to your magic!

In the end, our friend sold the diamond mine, gave most of the money to charity, married and had a family, went back to carpentry, and lived a comfortable and simple life until he died. Oh yeah, and he also occasionally taught seminars on how to enjoy and appreciate the magic in every moment of life and the Zen of carpentry, which was very rewarding.

The simple message of this book is to be aware of the inner world. Practice being alive in your soul. Expect a miracle in each and every moment. Expect magic to happen, look for it, and you will open to a world of unlimited possibilities. The magic of which this book speaks is obviously not to be confused with magical tricks of a sleight-of-hand artist. The magic of the soul is true spiritual alchemy— the art of transforming the world of form through the power of spirit. By opening to the magic of spiritual reality, we bring the magic of our souls into our everyday lives.

The magic of the soul is not something foreign or necessarily mystical. It is a natural phenomenon that we have all experienced in many ways. When we are relaxing on vacation, we may slip into a state of bliss, appreciating the beauty of life around us. When we witness the birth of a baby, we are in awe of the wonder and power of nature, of the Creative Principle of life. When we feel intense love or compassion for another being, we are naturally connected to our soul power. When we are challenged to dig deep into our being to find the courage to face a difficult situation, our soul power flows through us. When we create something that contributes beauty to our world, we do so through the magic of our souls. The practice of the magic of the soul is a process of deepening these experiences and making them more consistent in our lives.

Another synonym for magic is presence. The more we are aware of our surroundings, our internal processes (subtle sensations, emotions, and thoughts that condition our experience), our energy, and our soul influence, the more we will experience magic. We can recognize and experience the magic, sacredness, spiritual power in each situation we find ourselves. If the situation is pleasant, experience all the joy and wonder that is available in the moment. If the situation is unpleasant, painful, or even oppressive, allow yourself the freedom to feel pain, loss, or anger and also be present for the spiritual magic that exists within the situation itself. When we recognize the presence of the sacred, we automatically open ourselves to growth.

Spiritual magic exists in every experience whether we recognize it or not. Every experience leads us further along our path of evolution even if we are not aware of the growth. If we do recognize the magic, our experience of any event will be filled with much more power and freedom. When we look back on challenging moments, we usually recognize them as moments of intense growth. In retrospect, we may even feel blessed for having gone through them. My suggestion, or really, my echo of the ongoing suggestion from your own soul, from all souls, from the collective soul, is to recognize each blessing in the moment. Imagine how much more powerfully you will respond to a challenge if you accept it as a blessing, as a magical experience of growth, while embracing all the elements within you that are challenged. This practice is what I now call *radical gratitude*.

Be alert to the magic of life.

In many eastern disciplines, one traditional practice is to be non-judgmental. Finding the magic in every situation is a technique that can help us to accept whatever is happening in each moment. Seeing what we experience as magical creates a sense of vitality, which is one way I experience spiritual reality. There is a peace to the realm of the soul, but there is also a profound vitality.

Try experimenting with different terms or phrases that work for you. Try labeling a situation or condition as being filled with "spiritual power" or "potential for growth" or "sacredness." You can apply this strategy to any situation. I find it extremely useful for the "small stuff" that we get uptight about. If I drop something on my toe—instead of losing my temper completely or feeling the victim of fate—I may start to get angry, then catch myself and watch my reaction while choosing to see it as magical.

By seeing our experiences as magical or sacred we release our tension around them. Most of our tension and stress is the result of our resistance—resistance to pain or discomfort. By finding the magic in every moment, we can have greater appreciation for that which is enriching as well as a far greater potential for growth from that which is challenging. It must be emphasized that the goal is not to escape the pain (or any emotion), even though our experience of pain may be diminished significantly. In fact, we can go into the pain and experience the sacredness there. In doing so, we give up our resistance, look for the growth, and appreciate the wonder in every experience of life. We can feel our pain and other emotions at even deeper levels, freeing the energy in the emotion more fully and learning more from the experience.

Try this exercise: Every time you feel any kind of discomfort in the next week, whether it is the result of a conflict with someone, physical or emotional pain, or loss, use the discomfort as a cue. Let it be a reminder to you to look for the magic, sacredness, or opportunity for growth. See if the situation changes when you look at it from a deeper, more present perspective. If no deep awareness comes to you, you can still use it as a reminder to be present to your soul energy, to be the best you can be in that moment. In this way, every experience becomes an opportunity to go deeper into the true self.

Leading a magical life does not mean we will no longer have challenges. But through this practice, we can respond to challenge in a more powerful way and come to resolution much sooner and with healthier and more fulfilling results. At times, we may fail in our intention to practice this, as challenges may appear too overwhelming. But the more we recognize and experience the magic in every moment, even in retrospect, the more we reinforce an increasingly powerful and fulfilling existence. The longer we practice, the more ingrained and automatic the process becomes as we increasingly accept the truth of spiritual magic on a subconscious level.

When we are in the experience of appreciating the sacredness in life, we open to a world of unlimited possibilities. Because we are alert to the magic, we notice opportunities that we might otherwise miss. Opportunities stand out because we are looking for them and expecting magical experiences to occur. We find ourselves "in the right place at the right time." Life becomes filled with a deeper level of peace and meaning as we recognize every experience as something magical and know that each experience leads us to an ever-increasing expression of our soul energy.

Applied to a dramatic life experience, such as the death of a loved one, this practice can be more challenging and at the same time more rewarding. Chapter 9, Magic in the Dark, goes into this in greater detail. We can go into the intensity of our pain over loss and, believe it or not, find magic there. Contained at the heart of our pain is the magic of our love.

Kahlil Gibran expressed seeing the magic in every moment beautifully in this excerpt on pain from *The Prophet:*

> Your pain is the breaking of the shell that encloses your understanding.
>
> Even as the stone of the fruit must break, that its heart may stand in the sun, so must you know pain.
>
> And could you keep your heart in wonder at the daily miracles of your life, your pain would not seem less wondrous than your joy;
>
> And you would accept the seasons of your heart, even as you have always accepted the seasons that pass over your fields.
>
> And you would watch with serenity through the winters of your grief.[1]

APPRECIATING EVERY MOMENT

Nearly anyone who has survived a life-threatening illness emerges with a profound appreciation for life. The simple things that we sometimes take for granted can become profoundly valuable when threatened with the possibility that they may be lost. The ability to communicate and enjoy the company of loved ones, to grow and succeed, to play, to learn, to read, to smell a blooming flower are all priceless opportunities that we can be grateful for. We don't need to have our life threatened to appreciate these wondrous gifts. The farther along I travel on my magical path of the soul, the more I see these daily events as awesome privileges.

In the Carlos Castaneda series about his apprenticeship with a Yaqui Indian sorcerer, Don Juan constantly reminded Carlos to relinquish his self-importance and to use "death as an advisor." In *Journey to Ixlan*,[2] during his vision quest to "stop the world," he noticed a beetle crawling along a rock. While observing it, he had a realization. "The thought crossed my mind that death was watching me and the beetle." He recognized their likeness in that moment. "The beetle and I were on par. Our death made us equal." Our realization that we are no more important than any other being due to our mortality or any other reason can open us to the recognition that we are one with all beings, with all life. We can recognize that we are as beautiful as every other being. By using death as our ally or teacher, we can increase our appreciation for every moment and our sense of responsibility for utilizing each moment as an opportunity to grow.

Live life as though each moment is your last.

Recently, I asked this question at the dinner table with my family: "If you knew that the world was going to end in the next ten minutes, what would you say to me, to each other, in this moment?" We had a very profound conversation as each member of the family looked into their hearts for how they felt about the others. I recommend trying this sometime. Or when you are sitting with a friend and feeling the conversation is boring (which may be an indication that you are not seeing the magic in the moment), ask your friend what they would say to you if they knew they would die in a few moments. Ask yourself as well. It may open you up to a magical moment that is the potential in every moment.

We can also recognize the magic that is present in every loss. I know someone whose son was quite disappointed because he had lost a very lucrative contract for some office remodeling. Later, he considered it a profound blessing because had he gotten the contract, he would have been working on one of the top floors of the World Trade Center Towers on September 11, 2001. Is there a situation in your life where you are feeling a loss that may in fact be a blessing in disguise? We can give thanks for every situation with the understanding that we may not always see the hidden benefits.

What is beautiful in your life that is not being recognized in this moment? Imagine living life as an experience of awe and wonder. This is the magic of the soul. Is it possible to do this all the time? Maybe not, but then the question is, how much awe and wonder can you allow into your life in this moment? Practice letting more in on a consistent basis.

As you are reading this book, what is there that is magical in your life, in your immediate surroundings, in you? As you read this sentence, allow yourself to feel all that is magical about you and your life . . . feel your deepest love, your highest dreams, the beauty in your environment wherever you are, the growth you are experiencing from what is challenging you. Rest here on this page for a moment while you experience the fullness of your magical existence.

---

*Breathe deeply and feel the peace that is
available in this very moment.*

Recognize that in this state of peace you need nothing. . . . Now, from a position of needing nothing, ask yourself what you want in your life that would bring greater fulfillment and creative service to you and those you influence.

MAGIC IS EFFORTLESS

The belief that we benefit from struggle, that we must toil to get what we want, is a fallacy. If we want struggle, we should approach every goal from an awareness that it will be difficult to accomplish. If we choose magic, we will approach every goal with the belief that its accomplishment will be effortless. Try letting what you want come to you, rather than going after it. There are times when we learn through struggle, but ultimately the lesson we learn is that struggle is unnecessary.

About ten years ago, I taught a one-day workshop on subpersonality (unhealed aspect of the personality) integration, and I had an epiphany about my own patterns of struggle. I conducted and participated in a psychodrama involving role-play as a subpersonality interacting with other subpersonalities around an arts-and-crafts project. I acted out a stubborn subpersonality.

During the course of the exercise, a woman in the class innocently suggested that we build a structure with some of the materials that had been provided.

"Yes," I replied. "And we can build it all the way to the ceiling."

"No," she said. "That would be too difficult, we don't have to build it so high."

"Then why bother," I concluded.

In that moment, I recognized that all my life I had chosen goals that were nearly or even completely impossible. I needed to do something impossible to feel worthy, to accept myself, and to live up to my perception of the expectations of others and my internalized parental voice. Anytime I anticipated a task that would require learning a new skill, I would automatically expect it to be difficult. Of course, that expectation would usually be fulfilled. I suffered repeatedly by creating difficult projects to prove my worth or by making easy projects difficult out of a deep-seated belief that life was a struggle. There was a constant pressure I placed on myself to succeed and an ever-present but subtle accompanying fear that I would fail.

I had been working on letting go of struggle for some years before this epiphany. As a result of my ongoing work and a growing dissatisfaction with a life of struggle, I was ready to accept an easier, more magical way of living. The role-play was the catalyst for breaking out of the old mold and embracing a more powerful way of being. From that moment on, each time I would catch myself in the creation or expectation of struggle, I chose to switch it to one of simplicity—I would expect that the goal or task would be accomplished in an effortless and magical way.

As a result, my life changed miraculously over the next eight years. I went from earning a very modest wage for doing rewarding work in a stressful way to earning a six-figure income for doing rewarding work with less struggle. And I was empowering people by using spiritual principles through corporate management. But the truly magical transformation was the one that occurred within me: a continuing appreciation for the power of my own soul and a deepening of my inner path. There have been challenging moments through more recent years that have triggered my struggle tendency, but each one has helped to reaffirm that struggle is unnecessary. The tendency to create or expect struggle still crops up in subtle ways, but it no longer controls me, and I am able to access a more magical strategy almost instantly.

When I was first promoted to managing editor at Sage Publications, I applied the techniques of this philosophy to my business goals. The success that resulted was unprecedented in the company. The department I managed had been behind schedule for more than five years, and costs were increasing by about 10 percent per year. Within one year, the department forged ahead of schedule (and has remained there for eight years). On an annual budget of about $1 million, costs were reduced by 15 percent the first year and another 7 percent the following year. The total savings for the company over two years alone were over $350,000, which was calculated after bonuses were given to reward the staff who implemented the successful strategies. I was labeled a star manager in the company as well as one who empowered his employees.

When I was promoted to director and given responsibility for the production and printing of all publications, which included more than 200 books and more than 800 journal issues per year, my staff and I put systems in place that reduced printing costs by nearly $200,000 per year. Through my influence and the hard work of my staff members, the bottom line for the company was increased by millions of dollars over my eight-year tenure at Sage. While this success was the result of applying sound business practices, it would not have been nearly as effective without the application of sound *spiritual* practices. It was brainstorming, visualizing success both alone and with my staff (I taught these principles to them as well), praying for the right people to fill open positions, asking for spiritual guidance at every important decision, and giving thanks all along the way that actualized such a dramatic effect.

We can all create magical results in our lives by expecting the miraculous, asking for guidance, and visualizing success. Recognize that whatever you want can be achieved effortlessly, magically. Each time you contemplate a task, make the affirmation that it will be achieved with magical simplicity.

Claim your power.

MAGICAL CREATIVITY

You deserve everything in life that would be fulfilling to you, and accessing spiritual magic can manifest that which you desire that is truly fulfilling. Ask for what you want, but let go of any expectation that you will receive it. The process of asking and letting go is where the growth is to be found. If we look for results, then we are not practicing the magic of the soul. Magic depends on trust. Ask for what you want through prayer, visualization, and affirmation. Recognize how its fulfillment will benefit you and those you influence. Trust that how and when it manifests is in perfect harmony with all that is.

———————

Let it go.

———————

Be perfectly content without what you want and it will most likely find you. If it doesn't, something even more magical will. Continue to reaffirm that you don't need it. The more we accept the reality of each moment, the more peaceful we are inside. The more peaceful we become, the more power and the more energy we have to grow and manifest what we want.

Most of what we believe is possible or not is based on what we experience with our senses. Having joined the ranks of the great philosophers of the ages, modern science through quantum physics tells us that the *real* world—the world of energy (or one aspect of the real world)—is not at all what we perceive with our senses. We are all connected physically through energy as well as through spirit—although the latter has not been proven—yet. Our opportunity is to stretch beyond what we see, touch, hear, taste, and smell and to reach out to the real world. How do we do this? Experiment. Believe in that which seems improbable, even impossible.

Practice looking for the *energy* within the physical reality you perceive with your senses. Be aware of the quality of energy that moves outward from you. We are energy. We know this from a mental perspective. Practice making it real from the level of deeper intuition, feeling, and sensation. Let your mind and your beliefs become still, and at a subtler level intuit the oneness that we all are. As you are reading, feel the love that connects you to all life. See if you can feel a tingling sensation around your body as you become aware of the energy that connects you physically to all life.

Imagine yourself as a center of whirling energy, and as you move through the world, your energy blends with the energy of everything around you. The more positive your motivation and your intention in every situation, the more profound will be your influence on the world around you, and the more the world will feed back to you positive experience. Imagine that the energy around you is light, and when you add your positive intention to it, it is like a mist flowing outward through the light. The mist merging with the light creates a luminosity that is not present when the mist is not there. As human beings we have the opportunity to bring spiritual energy together with physical energy through our intent to integrate them.

By recognizing ourselves as energy, we can begin to operate in the world of form from a place of cause. When we identify as the energetic Creative Principle running through all life, we become more than the creation and part of the creating. Try approaching your goals and desires in life from a causal perspective. As creative energy you can create whatever you want. Don't hope for what you want. Intend what you want while appreciating everything you have.

---

*You are a spiral of loving light
flowing in all directions.*

The energy of our being is vibrating and therefore in constant motion and change, but we believe we are the same because we look and feel *relatively* the same. Affirm that you are a new person each day. The limitations you had yesterday do not need to exist in this new day. If they do crop up during the day, recognize them as continuing opportunities on your magical path of growth and affirm again in the moment that you are new and no longer need the same patterns. Will you get discouraged if you do not succeed each day or each moment? Only if you are looking for results instead of enjoying the magic of the process. And besides, if you persist, you will not fail. You will succeed at creating a new you. I guarantee it.

Practice recognizing and directing the power of your beliefs—your mental influence in the world. When I walked on hot coals at Stuart Wilde's Warrior's Wisdom Training as part of my research for an article for *Meditation* magazine, I had to step beyond my belief of what was possible.[3] I was able to reach a point where I *believed* I could do it. I know many have refuted the legitimacy of the fire-walk exercise, but I witnessed some who were burned, yet I and others were not. Why? Because we believed we could do it. If I had not learned to believe I could succeed before the walk, I am certain that I would have gotten burned. What is it in your life that seems impossible? Believe you can do it. See it happening in the energy beyond the level of sensory experience.

In some of my workshops, I teach people how to break boards, a skill I learned in kung fu training. It can be a great metaphor for breaking through blocks to achieve what we want in life. Standing there, facing a solid board that you have to break through, can bring up the same issues that hold you back from achieving your dreams in life. It usually brings up some degree of fear. If you fail, it will hurt your hand much more than if you succeed.

The keys to success are the following: 1) Focus your intent or will. You must have your power behind the action. 2) Concentrate. If you don't zero in on the center of the board, it isn't going to break. 3) Visualize your success. See it break before you strike. 4) Trust. Let go of your expectations and surrender to the process.

It is possible to break a board without succeeding at all of these steps, just as it is possible to achieve goals without succeeding at each step. By using these steps, however, the likelihood and quality of success is increased both in board breaking and in other accomplishments. The break will be cleaner and more painless. The accomplishment will be of a higher quality.

Any person of average strength can break a board if they hit its center, yet I have seen six-year-old children succeed and strong, 200-pound men fail. The greatest deterrent to success is fear. If we have a fear of failure, it clouds our focus and concentration. People do all kinds of misguided things out of fear. But to see the face of a sixty-year-old woman (or anyone for that matter) go beyond fear and break through the board is a pretty phenomenal experience. It is impossible not to feel the energy release that occurs, whether you are breaking the board or observing the event.

Experience the energy
release in everything you do.

One popular spiritual theory is that our need to grow is something that we should transcend. We should be present and let go of our desire to become more than we are in the present moment. I agree that life can only be lived in the present moment, but our inner desire to grow, to become more than we are, originates from our soul intention to evolve our personality. In the spiritual dimension there is no experience of past and future. Everything is happening in the now. But this doesn't mean there isn't a past and future. They just don't exist sequentially. Time is based on perceptual reality. So if we are truly present in the moment, we are including in that moment our past, our future, and our infinite existence.

Our desire to be more is one of the fundamental distinctions about being human and has led humanity to develop so quickly (in both healthy and unhealthy ways) over the past millenniums. Our desire for fulfillment is what inspires us to succeed. Desire is part of the formula for magical creativity. The trick to making our development healthy is how we utilize our desire to grow and in which direction we choose to move. The more we choose from our hearts, the healthier our choices will be.

Nearly every choice we make or action we take has two basic motives expressed in various degrees. We are motivated by some desire of our personality or ego and also from a higher motivation of our soul. For example: In teaching workshops or in writing this book, I am expressing my soul's desire to empower others, to spread light through the teaching. My personality also strives for success in order to realize practical values such as an income to meet my basic needs and provide for my family. My ego, which is an unhealed or less developed part of my personality, has needs such as recognition or self-importance. If we are successful at achieving our soul intent, it is in part because we have minimized the influence of our ego, and to some degree, our personality, and maximized the motivation from our souls. This is the basis of the practice of the magic of the soul or of any effective spiritual practice.

If we are driven by our ego or subpersonality needs for recognition and importance, then we will have great attachment to the outcome, because we will feel unimportant, perhaps even unworthy, if we don't succeed. We will have fear of failure. This is true, to a lesser degree, with regard to our personality needs for security. The more we are motivated by our spiritual, soul purpose, the more at peace we are with the outcome. If my soul purpose is to teach and empower people, it doesn't really matter if I reach one person or a million. It doesn't matter if I am an international spokesperson or if I am able to teach by setting an example through my interactions with my family and co-workers in a modest career. In practicing this philosophy, we can understand the relevance of the phrase, "Thy will be done." When we truly give our lives over to the magic of the soul, or to Spirit or God, we are content to serve in whatever way is presented to us as an opportunity.

This doesn't mean, however, that we should demean the personality or even the ego for its motivation. Spiritual growth or any growth is an ongoing process. We can recognize how far we have come in emphasizing the influence of the soul and de-emphasizing the influence of the ego. We can accept where we are and continue to strive toward greater growth. We can embrace our ego with compassion and understanding, for our weaknesses are the steps upon which our path of growth ascends.

One of the most important practices that I have embraced on my path is to accept myself the way I am and still desire to grow. This is a dichotomy, of course. When you reach a dichotomy, it usually means you are on the right track. The truth lies at the core of any dichotomy and contains the positive elements of both sides of the polarity. At the level of the personality, we see dichotomy, but at the level of soul, we experience wholeness. How can we love ourselves the way we are if we want to be more? If we try to understand it logically, we probably won't get very far. Try accepting that both ends of the polarity can be true even if it doesn't make sense to the rational mind. In fact, accessing the world of soul requires suspending rational thought. Not necessarily trying to eliminate it, but simply putting it in its proper place. Most of us tend to give more power to our minds than is effective. We can learn to use our minds as tools to accomplish the mission of our souls rather than using our minds to identify who we are. The secret is to recognize that we are more than our minds and to direct our thoughts from a soul-conscious perspective.

Recognize intuitively that you can accept yourself the way you are and affirm your continued growth. Be honest with yourself and accept exactly where you are in your spiritual growth, for it is part of the beauty of who you are. Practice appreciating everything you have on a physical level, recognizing that all of it is impermanent and that what is truly important is what you have inside you. Get to know that inner part more intimately.

Accept yourself completely.

Recognize that you deserve everything you want, yet there is nothing you need beyond what you have inside you. Strive for what you want with complete detachment from any results. This is another dichotomy that has tremendous power when it is embraced. It may take practice to let go of expectations, but the more practice you give it, the more effortless it becomes. Once we achieve a level of detachment, there is usually a larger desire or goal that will challenge us to higher levels of detachment. Focus your intent in the now and completely let go of any expectations for the future while you passionately declare with the full intent of your soul what you want from the universe.

Below is a formula for magical creativity. Use it to create whatever you wish in life.

1. *Visualize success*: Develop a clear picture in your mind of your accomplished goal. Include the feelings associated with the accomplished goal in your vision (see chapters 5 and 8 for more on affirmation and visualization). Ask for help from your spiritual guidance to create the right picture as well as to help you through the steps of accomplishment. Re-create your picture throughout the process as it evolves.

2. *Create an action plan:* Write down all the steps you will take and the resources you will need to acquire to accomplish your goal. Include personal resources such as determination, persistence, receptivity, love, etc. in your resource list.

3. *Implement the plan.* Take the steps that you have mapped out in your plan. Make sure you infuse the action with your emotion—the enthusiasm generated by the clear picture of the end result. Focus your intent to accomplish your goal. Be willing to do whatever it will take to reach success. Be aware of emotional issues that come up throughout the process, accept them, embrace them, and heal them (see chapter 6 for more on releasing and directing emotion).

4. *Let go and trust.* Let go of any expectation that you will accomplish your goal, and enjoy the process. Know that if you do not accomplish the original goal, something even more joyful and magical will come out of your efforts.

These steps are not necessarily sequential and can overlap and be repeated throughout the process. The following exercise is a visualization technique for manifesting goals. You can use this exercise in conjunction with the steps above for creating magical success in your life.

❊   ❊   ❊

Exercise for Manifesting Goals
(Track 2 on Audio CD)

Contemplate a goal you would like to achieve in your life. Close your eyes and breathe deeply. Feel your body become more relaxed with each breath. Get a clear image of your goal. Ask what might be standing in the way of that goal becoming real. Get an image of that block. See the image of the accomplished goal grow larger and brighter while the image of the block becomes smaller and faded. Link a symbolic physical sensation to the large, bright image of your accomplished goal, such as pressing two fingers together, touching your heart, or taking a deep breath. Ideally, it should be a physical act that you can perform in any setting. Affirm that you deserve your accomplished goal and that it will occur if it is healthy and good for you and others who will be affected by its accomplishment. Affirm that any time you have doubts or are confronted with a block to your goal that you will use your anchor to make its fulfillment real in the moment. Affirm that your goal has already been accomplished in mind and therefore exists in reality and will be manifested in the world of perception if and when it is what is best. Completely let go of any expectations about its accomplishment. Give thanks to your spiritual guidance for your accomplished goal. Feeling at peace, centered, loved, and empowered, take a deep breath and open your eyes.

❊   ❊   ❊

2

The Soul

Defining the soul is not an easy task. Everyone who has written on the subject has offered a different interpretation of the nature of the soul. Because it is something that is experienced from a level far more subtle than our normal means of perception, there is much room for interpretation. If two people are asked to describe a common object like a pen, they will usually come up with some consistent observations but also very unique ones based on their particular values and biases. So you can imagine the room for interpretation about something that is as nebulous as the soul. Because it exists at a level removed from time and space, any attempt at defining the soul using a vocabulary that is designed for describing the physical plane will only offer a glimpse of its reality. So it is far more useful to focus on ways of *experiencing* the soul than trying to understand it on a mental level or to validate its existence. While a definition can only indicate a glimpse, I will offer my own understanding of the soul here as a connection to the experiential content that is the heart of this teaching.

Everything I have ever read, heard, or experienced about the soul confirms that it is eternal regardless of the many beliefs about where eternity leads us. It is the essence, the center, the core of the human being. We talk about the individual soul—my soul, your soul—which does exist, but not in the sense that we understand individuality on the plane of perception. Even physical individuality is far more connected through energy than our perceptual experience of it. We know from the theories of quantum physics that what we perceive as solid objects are really particles of energy moving about in empty space. At an energetic level, we are completely connected to every other being and every other object through the energy and the empty space of which we are all composed. In many esoteric and metaphysical texts, this is called the etheric or causal world. The etheric plane and our etheric bodies are truer expressions of who we are and the reality within which we live.

The realm of the soul is even more connected, has less individuation, and of course is more subtle than that of physical energy. So when we experience life from the level of soul, we experience ourselves as one soul. The individual soul is more like a claim that our individual personality places on the collective soul.

It's kind of like the old proverbial question, if a tree falls in the forest and there is no one there to hear it, does it make a sound? Actually, it creates a vibration not a sound. Sound is the name we give to the sensory experience of hearing the activity of vibration. So it doesn't make a sound, but it creates an experience that can be perceived as sound. If the soul has no individual personality, is it individual? Yes, but it is a type of individuality that is far more subtle than our sensory experience of individuality in the same way that vibration is more subtle than sound. It would be difficult to distinguish the vibration of a tree falling from the vibration of a plane flying overhead, but the sounds are quite different. It is much more difficult to differentiate a soul from another soul beyond perception because all souls are inherently connected. The statement that "we are one soul" is more valid than the statement that "we have a soul." Kriyananda is a spiritual teacher and follower of Paramahansa Yogananda, the founder of the Self Realization Fellowship. He addressed this question by saying, "Our egos are nothing but vortices of energy that, within the vast ocean of consciousness, take on the appearance of a separate reality of their own."

The purpose of soul and spirit is to evolve matter. Because we are identified as individuals, soul individuates in order to help us evolve. Each individual soul is focused on the evolution or growth of the corresponding individual personality, but it is also involved in the evolution of all matter and of all personalities. So when we are soul conscious, we are naturally connected with everyone and everything as well as the process of growth in everyone and everything. The soul is also in direct contact with spiritual beings including angels and masters on the inner planes that are dedicated to aiding in the spiritual evolution of humanity and our planet.

Our soul or our true self is limitless, interconnected with all life, and immortal, yet we experience ourselves in the world of form as limited, separate, and imperfect. There are many dichotomies presented in this book because when we speak of the infinite, we do so within the context of the finite. Communication of this or any subject necessitates the experience of form and linear perception because language has evolved for the purpose of communicating in the world of form. But the goal of this or any truly valuable spiritual practice is to bring the two polarities together. We can honor our humanness as much as our spiritual nature and at the same time fuse them together through our practice. As we recognize and affirm the magic, the sacredness in our practical activities, they become more magical and limitless. Conversely, as our activities become endowed with our magical appreciation, they open us to higher levels of infinite understanding. Practicing the magic of the soul, therefore, makes our practical life more spiritual, our spiritual life more practical, and ultimately opens us to a spiritually practical existence.

---

*You are the bliss of spirit
and the vitality of matter.*

SOUL AS UNCONDITIONAL LOVE

As we touch the magic of our soul, we naturally experience ourselves as one with all life. We are immersed in unconditional love. It flows through us effortlessly. We not only experience it as enlightening and filled with wonder, but also as an intensification of what might be considered less desirable feelings. As we recognize our connection to everyone and everything, we care more about everyone and everything. Our compassion flowers as we feel the pains of others who suffer in the world. Our sadness increases over senseless violence. We become angrier at injustice. We can't help but be more outraged at the lack of care given to our environment, to the Earth— the mother from which we have all been born. We cannot have more love without having more compassion. As we let in more soul energy, the deepening of our emotional connection to the world is equaled by our ability to extend love and healing where we can make a difference. We become empowered by desire to manifest our soul purpose in the world. And we can recognize that all of the conditions of the world are part of the magical evolution of our planet.

As more love flows through us, we naturally have greater compassion and love for ourselves. This is essential, because we can't truly love anyone until we love ourselves fully. When we are immersed in the love of our souls, then love automatically fills us up and overflows outward and through others and everything. The excerpt below is a condensed version of a short story about spiritual growth, acceptance, and self love that I wrote and published in *Meditation* magazine.

Once upon a time, there was a far-off enchanted land called Anavrin. It was known as a place of peace. There was no war, disease, or struggle. Everyone worked and learned together in loving support. It is said that the sky was a multicolored kaleidoscope of pastel colors like waves of rainbows that filtered through the air, thick enough that they could be reached out for and touched.

In the center of this vast land was a small village named Pardisa. In this community lived a young girl named Kyla. Kyla was taught as a child about the place beyond Anavrin called ecstasy. She asked many questions of her teachers about this place, how and when she would get there, and what she would find. But no one knew any specifics, they just knew it was the next step toward something higher. They called it a graduation.

One day she had the courage to approach Hesham, one of the

village's elders. "Hesham, wise one," she said, "I feel your presence helping me when I sleep and when I am quiet. How is it you have the power to help people in this way?"

"How is it that you have the power to know what I am up to, Kyla?" he responded with a smile.

"Hesham, my teachers have told me that there are other forms of living and growing that are very different from those we have here. I desperately want to know about what they are."

Hesham smiled again, realizing he was in for a long conversation. "There are many other ways of life in this universe," he said. "There are even places where people fight against and harm each other. They do not recognize that they are part of each other as we do. Their children have two designated parents who teach them when they are young, instead of being raised by their community."

Kyla's eyes opened wide as she listened to such unbelievable stories. Her whole being quivered with anticipation as she asked the most important question. "What happens to us after this life? We live our whole lives learning and studying so we can reach another level that my teachers call ecstasy, but no one seems to know what it is like."

Hesham's smile faded slightly as he recognized Kyla's attachment to her need to know the answer. His eyes became like deep pools of water overflowing with wisdom. He spoke gently. "There is an old saying in Pardisa, 'The sky is always brighter on the other side of the rainbow.' It is valuable to question and seek knowledge about other realities, but it becomes an obstacle when it distracts us from living in the present. Life is a continuum. We are conscientious about learning our lessons not for the promise of ecstasy but to find use for our knowledge in the present and enjoy the process of development. Ecstasy is not out there in the future, Kyla. It is in your heart."

Kyla lived the rest of her life heeding the words of Hesham. She herself became a teacher of young ones and she relished every moment of her sacred time in the mystical land. When it was time for her graduation, the entire village held the customary ceremony. A great parade with Kyla at the front circled the village and wound around until it reached the altar at the center. Kyla laid on her back on the altar. Her closest friends circled the altar with the others behind them. She looked around at their smiles one final time before she closed her eyes.

Beams of golden light streamed from the outstretched hands of all the villagers surrounding and penetrating Kyla. The whole village chanted in rhythmic, soothing tones. She felt more peaceful than she ever had before. As the chanting increased in volume and intensity, she felt herself growing lighter. Her body slowly rose above the altar and she felt her consciousness becoming lighter and lighter. Finally, she disappeared from the view of her friends.

She found herself floating through a tunnel of light. She could but faintly hear the chanting and then it faded completely. She continued moving through the tunnel, yet there was no sense of space or time. As her consciousness began to merge with the light, she began to lose her sense of identity. Finally, she felt herself become the light, and then it was gone. Left was only darkness, no time, no space, no sensation. . . .

Then she felt movement again. She was in another tunnel and at the end of this one was a dull light. She moved through the tunnel with great effort, and the light became brighter as she approached the end. Suddenly, there was a sense of fear—an emotion she had never experienced—of the unknown. Then she heard muffled screams all around her as her heart raced with horrified yet excited anticipation. Then there was a burst of blinding light, clamoring noises, and giant awesome images. She was immersed in the experience of intertwined pain, fear, and the ECSTASY of being born into sensory experience in a far-off, magical land called Earth.[1]

As humans, we seek to become spirit. We strive toward a spiritual ideal. As souls, we seek to become human. We strive toward the evolution that is achieved through experiencing the imperfection of life in physical reality, the evolution of liberating or enlightening matter. As spiritual seekers, we could spend much of our lives striving for the peace of enlightenment and missing out on the exquisite privilege we have in being human. Our soul has longed to be human so it can learn and grow from the challenges of life. The pain, fear, and frustration as well as the ecstasy and triumph that are all part of being human draw our souls into physical incarnation so we as souls can evolve matter.

We reach for our soul to embrace perfection. This is called spirituality. When we arrive at our soul, we reach for our personality to embrace the splendor of our imperfection. This is called compassion. We see imperfection in ourselves and others as a beautiful opportunity, like parents who love their children not only in spite of their imperfections but because of them. It is the imperfections that make parents necessary in the growth of new life. It is the imperfections of physical existence that give soul its purpose. So when we view ourselves from our soul, we have supreme love, compassion, and understanding for ourselves and our journey of growth. This is why masters, saints, and magicians of the soul have supreme compassion for others. They understand the beauty of imperfection because they are viewing it from their souls.

As you read these words, allow love to wash over you. Let it flow through you in all directions. As though you have tentacles stretching in all directions infinitely, reach out to the world. Embrace all beings with the love and compassion of your soul. What if you maintained this awareness always? Impossible, you say? You are probably right. How could you maintain it more consistently? How would your life be different if you did?

---

*What is the limit of your ability
to love consistently, unconditionally?*

*Stretch for that limit and love yourself
when you fail at reaching it.*

The following exercise, designed by my psychosynthesis teacher, Dr. Vivian King, is a powerful technique for going deeper into the love of your soul and recognizing the purpose behind the challenges and peak experiences of your life.

※　　※　　※

Exercise for Loving Yourself
(Track 3 on Audio CD)

Close your eyes and view your life going backward. Remember the events of the past week, the past month, the past year. . . . Look over the important events of the past five years. Pay special attention to events that were particularly joyous or particularly difficult. . . . Continue moving backward in time over the previous five years. . . . Continue to move backward through your memories in five-year segments until you reach the time when you were an infant. . . . What was life like when you were age three or four? If you cannot remember, use your imagination. What do you think or feel it was like? How about at two years old? One? What was it like in the first week after you were born? What was your first day like? What was the first experience you had after being born? How did you feel leaving your mother's body? What was it like living in your mother's womb? How did you feel? Now go back to the time of conception. What was the purpose of your soul at that moment? Why did you choose your particular parents? What was your intent in choosing the challenges that you would face through your childhood, through your life? Imagine that you are your soul speaking to the present-day you. With the full compassion and love of your soul, tell your present-day self how you have done in growing through the challenges that you had set up to learn your lessons.

Write a letter as your soul to your present-day self, expressing your love and appreciation for all that the present-day you has gone through and encouragement for what is still yet to come.

When you have finished, put the letter in a self-addressed envelope, give it to a trusted friend, and ask him or her to send it to you when he or she feels the time is right.

❊   ❊   ❊

Loving yourself is a prerequisite, the first and most significant step in applying the magic of the soul. It is easy to love ourselves when we do really cool stuff—enjoy success in business, achieve an important goal, or impress a loved one. It is more difficult and the true test of self-love when we are challenged—when we file bankruptcy, are laid off, get divorced, or just plain screw up. Ultimately, we can look at these things as magical moments in our growth. The first step toward that level of acceptance is forgiveness.

Forgive yourself.

Accept yourself.

Love yourself.

THE SOUL AS POTENTIAL

The soul is a balance of the qualities that make up our ideal self, our potential. Our potential is to be balanced in all transpersonal qualities. Transpersonal qualities include all of our ideals and spiritual values. While there are many such qualities, there are three basic transpersonal qualities that can give us clarity about our potential in the world: will (or power), love, and creativity. Because of the limitations of a language designed to describe physical reality, these words have limitations in interpreting and describing transpersonal qualities and are only approximations of the splendor of soul reality. The following are synonyms that may help clarify the ideas, but realize that even these can only point toward true clarity, which must be experienced.

Will: power, force, direction, intent, cause, initiating principle, masculine energy.

Love: receptivity, nurturing, compassion, tenderness, openness, magnetic attraction, feminine energy.

Creativity: product of interactions between will and love, birth, action, magic, idea in form, integration of masculine and feminine.

Will, love, and creativity are the three basic qualities of life and are representative of the trinities that run through most world religions. In Christianity, it is the Father, Son, and Holy Spirit. In Hinduism, there is Shiva, Vishnu, and Brahma. Hebrew scholars learn about Kether, Kochma, and Binah. Buddhists take refuge in the Buddha, Dharma, and Sangha. In ancient Egypt there was Ra, Osiris, and Horus. New Thought metaphysics speaks of Spirit, Consciousness, and Matter. Native American tribes call them the Grandfather, Grandmother, and all of life is their children. All of these trinities illustrate and emphasize different variations and degrees of influence of the three transpersonal qualities of will, love, and creativity. I could go into detail about how the three qualities manifest in each trinity, but we can gain more clarity, I think, by looking at how these three are portrayed in nature.

The Creative Principle is a trinity. Every creation has three forces operating in the creative process. There is the masculine (will), the feminine (love), and the creation (that which is born out of the interaction between the feminine and masculine energy). Whether we are talking about the birth of a child, the flowering of a plant, or the blooming of an idea, they are all a product of this magical Creative Principle. This is the blueprint for all of creation as well as the nature of God the Creator. We were created in God's image, so we too contain the will, love, and creative expression in various proportions and levels of development.

Usually people are strong in one aspect and weaker in others. The willful businessman or politician is sometimes lacking in love and compassion. The compassionate humanitarian is sometimes lacking in will or power. When these two are well developed and balanced, then the development and balancing of creativity is usually quite easy as it is the product of the first two.

If these qualities are not balanced, we will receive experiences to help bring them into balance. Most people who are considered geniuses are those who have a high degree of balance between the three transpersonal qualities. If Einstein did not possess a high degree of will (the force that inspired him to research and develop his theories), love (a receptive force that opened him to an understanding that superseded physical reality), and creativity (the force that allowed him to present his findings in a form that was received by his peers and the world), he would not have been nearly as successful. He likely would not have been considered a genius, and we probably never would have heard of him.

A willful person with little love generally seeks out powerful positions in life, often without thought about who or what they may trample to reach their goals. They create success that brings back little rewards in terms of nurturing or love, because they offer little in this area themselves. Willful people who are ready for spiritual growth will eventually, through their successes and failures in life, recognize that there is something missing and begin searching for ways to receive, develop, and express more love.

A loving person without much power will spend much of their energy nurturing others with little focus on themselves. Extreme co-dependence characterizes the loving person who lacks will. If they are ready to evolve further along their spiritual journey, they will eventually choose to become more powerful, create stronger boundaries, and become advocates for themselves. This allows them to become more effective in their love as they generate self-love, which then overflows into more genuine loving action toward others.

The creative person who is lacking will creates in a way that will have little effect on life. The creative person who is lacking love can be the most destructive (especially if they also have a well-developed will) because they have the capacity to create things and situations that are effective but most likely are not supportive of others or the betterment of the planet. Weapons of mass destruction are examples of will and creativity without love.

Will is the pure force of spirit manifesting in all forms. It is the energy of initiation or first cause. Creativity is birth and regeneration of spirit in form. Love is the quality that holds it all together. It is the magnetic force that connects all life whether in physical or spiritual form. The soul contains the balance of these three energies. We can facilitate the balancing of the three energies by recognizing where we are deficient and by working to develop that particular quality. Life and our soul intent guides us toward this balance, but if we participate more consciously, it speeds up the process.

Assess which of the transpersonal qualities you express the least in your daily activities and long-term goals, and consciously strive to express them more fully. How would your activities change with more balanced expression? Look for ways to consciously apply the three transpersonal qualities in a balanced expression and notice the effects. By doing so you will greatly facilitate your growth and your ability to appreciate and create magic in your life.

When we are in alignment with our soul through meditation, conscious intent, or simply surrendering, we are naturally in a state of greater peace and are more balanced between will, love, and creativity. We can become immersed in a perspective that goes beyond any sensory experience of life. An experience that threatens our personality may pull us out of that state, but we can choose to move back into it. The act of choosing surrender is one that requires both will and love. When we blend will with love we are not only surrendering but consciously choosing to be love in action. We can purposely infuse our environment with love through our will or intent to do so.

Our soul guides us by consistently radiating qualities of divine will, love, and creativity (and many other related transpersonal qualities). As our personality grows, it naturally opens more and more to the vibration of the soul. We can greatly facilitate our spiritual evolution and a balanced expression of soul by being receptive to that radiance and consciously choosing to access soul energy. When we do, we feel empowered. Later chapters will delve further into practical ways of accessing and applying soul energy. For now . . .

---

open to your radiance.

Our world today illustrates a collective personality that is strong in will and creativity but lacking in love. Our collective mind (which is related to the will and to some degree creativity) has developed faster and with more influence than our collective heart (which relates to love). Humanity is at a point where it is ready to balance its energy, to develop the area that is lacking by growing in its ability to receive, develop, and express more love. If we continue along our present path of willful creativity—increasing technology without sufficient concern and nurturing for our mother earth and for the well being of all life—we may destroy ourselves.

But the nature of growth is a process of balancing. Some people believe we will destroy the planet if we don't change our ways. Fortunately, we are not powerful enough to accomplish such an act. Peace on earth will be achieved, but it is up to humanity whether or not we will be around to enjoy it. If we do bring about an environmental holocaust, it will most likely not destroy all of humanity, just enough to bring the planet back into balance and allow it to heal. The survivors will then start over with the knowledge gained from the effects of the cataclysm and hopefully move forward with greater wisdom and, of course, love. Everything balances in the end; it is just a question of how much we choose to cooperate with the balancing that makes the ride a treacherous or joyful experience. So part of the influence of the soul, whether the soul of a planet or an individual, is to guide the personality through the experiences the soul provides to a greater balance of the three basic transpersonal qualities. In simpler terms, to grow.

Below is an exercise that can greatly facilitate integrating and balancing transpersonal energy by meditating on ancient symbols representing will, love, and creativity. In recent history, the system was developed and tested in the 1940s by a psychologist named Dr. Viola Neil. Experiments were done with psychiatric patients in three groups for a period of one year. The first group was asked to do nothing but meditate on three symbols: a circle with a dot at the center for will, an equal-armed cross or plus sign representing love, and a triangle representing creativity. The second group underwent therapy. The third group did nothing. As would be expected, the second group reported a healthier outlook and increased fulfillment in life than the third. It was expected that the first group would approach the success of the second but, in fact, the symbol meditators surpassed the success of those being treated traditionally. The first group reported a healthier outlook and greater fulfillment and success in life than the second group.

A number of the individuals who participated in training classes by Dr. Neil went on to become major leaders of various spiritual movements including: Dr. Earl D. Barnum who was one of my early teachers, one of the founders of Religious Science, and the founding minister of the Redondo Beach Church of Religious Science, and Dr. Robert Gerard who was a pioneer in the field of Psychosynthesis (a transpersonal therapy) and the founder of Integral Psychology (psychology of the spirit). There are many other well-known leaders, as well as less-famous individuals, who went on to have significant impact on the lives of others by realizing their potential through this simple technique.

I believe that much of what I have accomplished in my life, including the writing of this book, would not have occurred if it weren't for my practice of meditating on these symbols for prolonged periods of time. I hold this practice responsible for my ability to reach into the depths of spiritual understanding and at the same time be able to create and manage an annual budget consisting of over $4,000,000 at the height of my career as corporate director. Without this practice, I would have still done well with the former but would have definitely struggled with the practical elements of financial management.

Meditation on Symbols

For free audio version, http://www.livingpurposeinstitute.com/meditation.htm

*Take a few deep breaths and relax. Imagine that emerging in front of your third eye, the point between and slightly above your eyebrows, is a circle with a dot at the center, representing Divine Will. Imagine that you are being filled with Divine Will. See the symbol as white against a black background. Imagine that the dark background is a canvas with a cutout of the circle with the dot, and that light is shining through the image. Try imagining that rather than you holding the symbol in place, the symbol, or Divine Will, is holding **you** in place. After five minutes, allow the circle with the dot to fade and be replaced by an equal-arm cross or plus sign. Feel yourself being filled with Divine Love. After another five minutes, replace the plus sign with an equilateral triangle, representing Divine Creative Action—the ability to manifest. Imagine yourself being filled with Divine Creative Action. After five minutes, close by reflecting on how a balanced expression of will, love, and creativity can be expressed in your life.*

Note: It is recommended that to get the full effects of this practice, you do this exercise on a daily basis for a minimum of nine months. If you miss a day, you then add one day to the nine months.

KARMA

The soul does not judge anything as good or bad because every experience can and will produce growth over time. Many spiritual doctrines preach nonjudgment but subtly sneak judgement in between the lines. In many eastern interpretations, karma is portrayed as a form of punishment just like hell is in western doctrine. Many Judeo/Christian thinkers, even those in traditional denominations, no longer profess a fiery inferno as an afterlife for evildoers. One rapidly growing alternative in theological thought is the recognition that heaven and hell are metaphors for states of consciousness or experience created through our actions. Karma also has a more empowering interpretation as a positive force inspiring growth.

Karma is the Creative Principle working according to natural law. Karma is soul force influencing the physical plane or the arena of form. Karma does not punish; it provides opportunity for growth. This is not just semantics. There is an important distinction. The soul does not punish. God does not punish. God is the Creative Principle and therefore can only create—not destroy. Destruction of form occurs, but even this is part of the creation because everything that dies in the world of form supports and becomes part of life in another form. In physics, the axiom is "energy can never be created or destroyed." It simply changes form. Plants die and become compost for other plants. Animals become food for humans. All flesh becomes fertilizer for other life. In a metaphysical sense, humans are food for the soul. Our lives and deaths, triumphs and failures nourish the soul in its quest to enlighten matter.

In terms of karma, if we continue to miss a lesson that will lead to a higher expression of our soul, we will be presented with that lesson in different forms until we learn the lesson. If we steal something, our karma may not necessarily be that someone will steal from us, but our action of stealing is a testimony that we need to learn a more powerful way of being. Our actions, our souls, and the Creative

Force of the universe will present life circumstances that will pro-vide the opportunity to learn the value of not stealing. It may come in the form of losing the item we stole or an even more important item. It may come in the form of someone close to us being stolen from. It is likely that the form will be the lesson that will most like-ly bring results.

Every action creates a reaction, but we cannot know what that reaction will be. It is not that calculated but it is persistent. It is like-ly that the longer we resist a lesson, the more difficult the challenges inspiring us to learn it will become. We may lose someone close to us as a result of a stealing incident. For example, my partner could get killed in the process of the heist. Being caught and going to jail can teach us the lesson. Or even the threat of going to jail might do it for some. The point is, once we truly learn the lesson, there is no need for further karmic debt. In John Lennon's song, "Mind Games" (which is about spiritual transformation and service), one of the lyrics is "putting our soul power to the karmic wheel." This means that when we truly learn our lesson, we have infused our personali-ty with soul power. Not only will we no longer steal, but we will teach others the importance of generosity. We may be drawn into cir-cumstances with those from whom we have stolen (possibly in future lives) to balance the energy. It doesn't necessarily mean that they will steal from us or that they will get something that was stolen from us or that we will be punished. It may mean that we will assist them in some way. It may mean that they will benefit from the lessons we have learned about integrity.

If we know the right path or even have an intuition about what is right but choose another path—our ensuing experience will clari-fy that our initial understanding was correct. If we choose the high road, it is because we were ready to empower ourselves toward a higher level of soul expression. If we choose the low road, we learn through our experience the value of the high road. One is not better than the other. The universe and our soul do not care how long it takes us to evolve, although the support toward growth is present in every moment. But when we choose the high road, the experience is richer and more joyful. With each moment that we choose the light of our soul, we build momentum toward soul/personality fusion.

Deepak Chopra writes about time and the magnetic pull of the soul in his book *How to Know God: The Soul's Journey into the Mystery of Mysteries.*

> No one makes the soul journey faster or slower than anyone else. Time doesn't count at the level of soul. What counts is perception. When you perceive that awakening is inevitable, the magnetic pull of the soul will keep changing you.[2]

Love yourself through your difficult lessons. Forgive yourself when you don't choose the easiest path. Look for the magical growth available in every experience. I offer two guidelines for choice in right action, neither of which are mine. The first one is

---

"Do unto others as you would have them do unto you."

What a simple and powerful instruction to follow in every situation. These words offered by Jesus Christ are almost self-evident, but how often are they ignored or subjugated to rationalization. We may believe in the message but not practice it in all situations. "It doesn't apply to this situation." Or we simply don't ask the question, "Am I treating this person in a way that I would like to be treated by others in this moment?" Imagine the state of the world if everyone practiced this instruction with diligence. Ask yourself before you act, "Is this how I would want someone to act toward me in this situation?"

"Act with impeccability."

This phrase was stated repeatedly by Don Juan in the Carlos Castaneda books, which is another way of saying the same thing as do unto others. It means with every choice, act in a way that creates more power for you and everyone who is affected by the choice. How could anyone ever make a wrong choice with this intention?

WIN-WIN

I want to be clear about my stance on future and past lives. I believe in reincarnation because I have remembered my own past lives through various meditative experiences and because it is a theory that makes sense to me. But I admit that these experiences could be manifestations of my own subconscious. I am also sensitive to the fact that reincarnation is contradictory to many western religious beliefs, and as such, I present it as a personal belief but not one that is necessary to embrace in practicing the message of this book. In fact, there is no belief that should stand in the way of this practice or any other that you find helpful in your spiritual journey. It does seem likely to me, however, that we are going to be given more than one opportunity to get it right here. I certainly hope so.

DIRECTING FROM THE SOUL

Later chapters in this book ask you to observe the functioning of your mind, emotions, and body—to recognize that you can choose how you want to direct each of these functions of your personality. If you are more than your body, feelings, and thoughts, who are you? Who *is* the you that can observe your physical, emotional, and mental bodies? Who *is* the you, the center, that can choose how you wish to express the magic of your soul?

Stop reading and close your eyes. Observe your body, emotions, and mind and then ask who is doing the observing?

Meditate on your center . . .
the self . . . YOU.
Practice being your center . . . the soul.

When we are centered in personality or form awareness, we are looking at life from the inside out—everything we experience is filtered by our personal biases. Life reflects back to us exactly what we expect from it based on our belief systems. It is our thought process that holds our experience of reality in place. It takes energy to hold the perceptual world in place. When we release that hold, we free up more energy for magical creativity.

When we are centered in soul awareness, we can view any person, place, thing, or circumstance from the outside in. We contain an understanding that can only be found in the space outside our individualized awareness. Practice approaching any situation or observation from the awareness of your soul.

It is the interplay between our fixed universe and unconditioned reality or soul awareness that determines our progress on our path of evolution. The intention to express life from the level of soul bounces back and forth against the patterns of the personality, and with each bounce, the ball of expanding consciousness goes higher, gaining momentum with an exponentially increasing velocity of soul impact on our form. When we contact spirit and experience a higher ideal, our personality is challenged to integrate that higher ideal.

For example, you may have an insight that you can empower your children by relating to them with more kindness and less anger. You may make the commitment to raise your voice at your kids only as a means of getting their attention when they aren't listening and never as a form of criticism, but you find it difficult to put into practice or to draw a clear line. Your desire to achieve that intent is a reflection of soul alignment. But your own habits, which are based on your experiences as a child and your consistent reinforcement of them throughout your life, create a polarity between your intent and practical application. You continue to try but find yourself falling back into old patterns, especially when you are under stress.

The more you approach your goal consciously, the faster will be your progress at achieving it. If you make the intent to not criticize but get caught up in your fears or worries, then criticize without thinking, then put it out of your mind because you don't want to deal with it, your progress will be slow indeed. You may even give up for a time. But the fact that you have recognized the value of growing in that direction guarantees that you will, no matter how long it takes or how many times you start over.

If you approach it more consciously, carefully observing the effects of success or failure, then every time you fail, you will feel the discomfort of the failure and be increasingly reminded of the discomfort it creates for your children. You will be drawn to greater determination to succeed through the interplay between whatever blocks are keeping you from succeeding and the increasing presence of your soul intent. In this scenario, your progress will be much faster and can even happen magically, with lasting results.

As we practice being the soul and radiating love, a tension is created between striving for a higher ideal and holding onto familiar patterns. This tension is part of the growth process. Bless your struggles to grow as well as your times of peak spiritual awareness.

Throughout this ongoing process of evolution, we can at any moment take quantum leaps. Through our intention and letting go of our personal identification—our accepted limitations—we can apply soul power to the karmic wheel. We can open and live in the moment of the magic of our souls.

---

*You are a soul having
having a human experience.*

3

Applying Magic

One of the magnificent things about the dynamic of a spiritual practice is that it is just that—a practice. When we practice any skill, we are usually more relaxed than when we are performing the skill "for real." The athlete practices so that the game-time performance is enhanced. The writer practices in order to accomplish greater creativity in writing projects. If we make an error while practicing, it's okay, we were "just practicing." It is helpful to have this same relaxed attitude about spiritual practice. By doing so, we can strive for a high ideal without judging ourselves when we do not reach it.

Our success at applying the magic of the soul can be assessed by how often we feel at ease and empowered as well as how often we empower others. The average person spends most of their day in a state of tension—for some it is intense tension and for others it is more subtle. That tension usually manifests in behavior that is less than healthy for ourselves and others, including hurrying at a frantic pace, giving ourselves negative internal messages, and snapping at others. It is one thing to affirm that magic exists in every moment, and it is another to live it consistently.

In contemplating how to overcome the obstacles to living a magical life, we come to another dichotomy. While transformation happens instantaneously at the level of soul, it appears to take time on the physical plane. If our intention is to radiate the magic of our souls on a regular basis, we *will* achieve that goal. Since we will achieve it in time and space, it has already happened in timeless, spaceless spiritual reality. But in the world of appearance, we may need to go through a *process* that makes it manifest in form. It may take years or lifetimes, or it may happen right now in this moment if you are ready for it.

Are you enlightened yet?
If you answer no, how can you be sure?
Stop and answer this question thoughtfully.
Then try letting go of the answer.

Try letting go over and over again of the self-concepts that keep you from realizing your essential divinity, your magical capability. Once we have committed to the goal of being a positive force in the world—what is often called being on a spiritual path—every experience will lead us toward that goal. Even our greatest failures at being that positive force help us to move further into the accomplishment of the goal. If we resist making the choices that will further us along the path, we will be presented with experiences that will inspire us to choose more wisely the next time.

The further along the path you are, the stronger will be the experiences that motivate you toward success. That is how the soul and karma work together. For those who have committed to their soul intent but still resist it in conscious or unconscious ways, it may require a life-changing event—sickness or an accident—that forces (or inspires in a powerful way) the individual to a deeper awakening, to a deeper connection with the soul. Or such events may happen as a choice of the soul to speed up the growth process.

I have been consciously on a path for over twenty-seven years. It has been my intention all these years to live and teach peace and love. I found it difficult to succeed in many situations. It wasn't until

I became very ill a few years back that I was inspired (it felt like I was being forced) to transform on a deeper level. I was so ill that I was not able to work or exercise or even carry on a conversation at times. In order to heal, I had to reach a deeper point of inner peace. My nature throughout my life has been characterized by nervousness, some of which is the result of subtle fears. Years of emotional healing and spiritual practice have greatly transformed these tendencies, but they still exist on subtle levels and continue to inspire further growth. My illness was a direct result of my fears having to do with emotional loss, physical stress from a demanding job, and some genetic deficiencies that were later diagnosed. I had lost a love relationship after a long period of emotional and physical stress and a lung infection turned into a long-term case of Chronic Fatigue also exacerbated by active Epstein-Barr virus and other factors. Ongoing fears that I would not live up to the expectations of others, fears of being alone, fears of not being worthy or good enough, and ultimately fears of ongoing illness and even death all contributed to the ongoing symptoms.

My chronic illness lasted over two years and became so debilitating that there were times I could barely walk or get out of bed. If I ran a few steps to answer the phone, I might be laid up for weeks. Talking and even laughing was painful. There were times when I thought I was dying, and maybe I was. Throughout much of the illness, there was no clear medical diagnosis, so I often thought I was crazy or it was all in my head. The only way I could make slow progress was to maintain a state of peacefulness at all costs. My body became a perfect biofeedback device by letting me know when I was disempowering myself or others. Everything that I held onto as a sense of ego identification was removed during this time, including my athletic body, the physical energy that fed my charisma, my ability to influence others in dynamic ways, and my ability to perform my corporate responsibilities (to which a significant part of my identity had become attached). It seemed that I had no choice but to go deeper within and discover at an intense spiritual level who I was beneath my personality. I had to learn ultimate trust and detachment because I could not heal as long as I held onto my personality needs to heal. I had to continually let go of all fear and frustration. I could have chosen another path—continued illness or death—but I vowed to do whatever it took to be healed. I learned to experience my illness as a blessing, as a magical intervention of my soul leading me to a fuller expression of its intent.

I emerged a healthier person on many levels, one who was motivated and proficient at holding the presence of my soul. I learned that nothing was more important than the inner presence. I learned to accept my experience as a blessing even in moments of extreme pain or despair. Not that I didn't resist as I was learning to give up resistance and not that I don't still resist at times. But the only way I could progress in my healing was to let go and trust. I often think that anyone who hasn't gone through such a challenging experience is at a disadvantage, but I also realize that I didn't have to go through the struggle. It was the choice of my soul to create a burning ground for many of the blocks that I still held onto.

I could have chosen an easier path, one that did not offer the amount of discomfort I chose to progress on my path. But this represents another example of that familiar dichotomy. In a way, I had to choose it because I did choose it. We always have choice, but if we choose a more difficult way to learn, it is because we need (or want to from a soul level) to learn the lesson in a more lasting way. This reinforces the truth that echos through the pages of this book that there is magic in every experience, in every lesson.

Once we reach an ability to create a positive vibration in our environment on a consistent basis, it can become effortless. As with many goals, especially those related to consciousness, we look back and say, how easy it is now. How could I have ever chosen such limitation and fear when freedom was there all along waiting for me? Awakening happens in the moment, and it is up to us when we want that moment to be realized, and it won't happen any sooner than we are ready for it. But our consistent affirmation and practice of choosing magically, effortlessly, will hasten our readiness and manifestation of the process of enlightenment.

Gautama Buddha told his disciples that they didn't need to go through the struggle he did to achieve enlightenment. It was there all along, but the freedom came by experiencing its opposite. How much struggle do you require to realize that you don't need it?

Be as a river.

The magic of the soul is like a river. It flows from the highest point to the lowest, bringing life and sustenance to all it touches. It does not judge or choose the direction of its current but winds through the path of greatest simplicity with power, tenderness, and freedom.

Be as a river.

While we are walking on the path toward greater freedom and power, it is helpful to assess where we are on the path, how far we have come and how far we have to go, always realizing that there is no place more important than right where we are. The following exercise is a very powerful technique that I learned from my teacher, Dr. Vivian King. It utilizes symbols or archetypal representations to clarify subtle aspects of the personality and psyche as a self-assessment. It can reveal areas of strength as well as those in need of development. The more time you spend exploring each area and the inhabitants of the castle, the more information you can receive about yourself. You can further benefit by clearly identifying different characters living in the castle. Look for details in each of the rooms you explore. Each time you do this exercise, you may receive an entirely different experience depending on your state of mind and increased growth since the previous journey.

❋   ❋   ❋

The Magician of the Soul
(Track 4 on Audio CD)

Allow your body to slowly come to a point of complete physical relaxation. Your emotions come to a point of calm. Your mind rests at a point of still peace.

Imagine that you are walking through an enchanted land and ahead of you is a castle. The castle represents you. What does it look like from the outside? What are your first impressions? Walk to the castle and enter through the main entrance. What is it like inside? Explore the various rooms in the castle. What is the greeting room like? Is it warm and inviting? Is it foreboding? What objects are in the room? Does the furniture look comfortable? What about the kitchen? Is there ample food for all the inhabitants? Walk through the corridors and find the master bedroom. Is this room comfortable? Is it a room that is conducive to creative dreaming? Is the bed comfortable and inviting? Explore any other areas of the castle that are appealing to you. Who are the inhabitants in this castle? Are the people friendly? Who runs the castle? Is it run justly, with kindness, or are the laws confining? Now find the door to the dungeon. Put your hand on the door handle and see if you can imagine what is inside. Is the door locked, and does it need a key to get inside? Open the door and walk down the steps. What do you see? Is this a dark and gruesome dungeon? Has it had renovations, and is it cleaned regularly? Does it stay locked most of the time? What secrets are kept in this place? Allow yourself to be open to what is held in the darkness. Is there a way for light to get into the dungeon? What does this place need to become lighter? Now make your way to the highest tower in the castle—the place of greatest light. What is this room

*like? How much light exists here? Is this room often visit-
ed, or is it dusty from lack of use? How can the light from
this room be integrated into the dungeon? Open your eyes
and draw or write down your experience of the castle.*

*When you are through writing, close your eyes again
and imagine that you are back in the castle. Now walk to
the highest tower and look in the closet. Here you find a
magical gown, cape, and wand. Dress yourself in the gar-
ments. These are your clothes—the clothes of the magician
of the soul. As the magician in the tower, take a good look
at your castle. Decide what it needs to be healthier—a
more perfect reflection of the magic of your soul. Take your
wand in hand and begin to symbolically renovate your castle. Change any deficiencies that you assessed on your tour.
You are the magician, and you can do years of work in a
matter of seconds, effortlessly and with dynamic results.
Clean the dungeon if it is in need. Create a method of illuminating the darkness. Give your castle whatever it needs.
Create the ideal system of government and call together all
those who live within its walls—all those different aspects
of your personality. Tell them that there is a new regime,
that the castle will be run by the light of the soul and that
you, the magician, are responsible for guiding that light.
Wave your wand and create peace and love throughout
the land. Open your eyes and once again write what you
experienced.*

☀   ☀   ☀

Some of the impressions you received during this exercise may
give you instant insight, and others may become clearer over time. I
suggest going over your notes in a week or two and see if more is
revealed.

When interpreting symbols, it is helpful to remember that there are some universal generalizations that can be made, but the most important criterion for interpretation is what the symbol means to each individual. With this in mind, the following are some guidelines for universal generalizations that can be applied to the individual experience.

The castle represents the entire self, including subpersonalities, the lower unconscious or shadow, and the higher self or soul.

The greeting room to the castle can be symbolic of how you present yourself to the world. Is it warm and inviting or foreboding? The answer can indicate how you present yourself to the world.

The kitchen can symbolize nourishment. A lack of ample food could mean a need for more self-nourishment or nourishing of others.

The master bedroom can be symbolic of self-relationship or relationship to the unconscious as it is the place where sleeping takes place.

The other rooms can mean different aspects of self—states of mind or emotional moods.

The inhabitants or the people living in the castle can be different aspects of the self or subpersonalities. A subpersonality is an unhealed or underdeveloped aspect of the personality that is formed in childhood because of a particular unmet need. The result is unhealthy emotions or behavior patterns.

The ruler, or the one who runs the castle, can often be a subpersonality rather than the soul or the soul-conscious self. Who runs the castle often determines whether it is run justly, efficiently, or healthfully.

The dungeon represents the lower unconscious or shadow self and contains unconscious or repressed emotions—pain, anger, or fear—and has its roots in the past. People who have examined themselves through therapy or other means will often have cleaner, lighter dungeons than those who have not done as much internal work.

The highest tower represents the higher self or the soul. Integrating the light from the tower into the dungeon represents bringing the light of the soul into the lower unconscious. Many systems teach transcending the fears, pain, and anger of the personality in favor of the light of the soul. This method suggests bringing them together—illuminating the shadow with the light of the soul.

The magician of the soul is the soul-conscious personality that is adept at applying spiritual magic in the world of form.

HABITUAL MAGIC

We are creatures of habit and a great deal of difficulty in transforming is due to the internal habits that drive our behaviors. But we can use our habitual tendencies to our advantage. Practice making transformation a habit. Use cues throughout the day to remind yourself to consistently recognize the sacredness in life. Create cues that will remind you to come back to center, such as every time you walk through a doorway, remember the sacred. If you work at a computer all day, every time you go into a new program or minimize or maximize a screen, come back to your center. Eventually the habit of presence will replace the unconscious habits that condition your life.

Another method for making presence more consistent is to act as an objective observer. Any time you find yourself acting in a way that is inconsistent with your soul intent, step back and observe yourself. Look for the feeling, the reason you are acting the way you are. Learn from the experience. At the earliest possible point, choose to change your behavior. Be careful not to repress your feelings in this process. If you can't change the behavior without repressing, then give your emotions the expression they need to release. Cry or scream if you need to, but observe yourself as you do and recognize the magic in your feelings.

You will learn more from the results of your emotional reaction if you observe the process and the cause than you will if you try to suppress it. Ultimately, suppression doesn't work because it will only build up, become stronger, and lead to an even greater reaction later. It could even cause illness as the energy becomes blocked and internalized. The result of observing your reaction in any situation will inspire you toward a stronger commitment to act in accordance with your intent—the intent of your soul.

If your spouse or partner ridicules you, you may experience hurt or anger. It likely will remind you (consciously or unconsciously) of the critical voice of a parental figure that you have internalized and oftentimes use to ridicule yourself with internal dialogue. Watch your response during and after your reaction. If you are angry, look for the hurt or fear. There is always a deeper emotion beneath anger. Don't judge yourself, but decide in the moment how you would like to have responded. Share the deeper feeling with the person with whom you are in conflict. Come from your vulnerability so that both of you can learn from the encounter. When you come from anger, you put people on the defensive, which usually turns into an offensive. When you shift to vulnerability, you disarm others and usually inspire them to go to their vulnerability as well. Vulnerability draws individuals together. Attack creates separation.

As we learn from the reactions that are inconsistent with our desire to apply the magic of our souls, eventually we will less frequently look outside ourselves to get our needs meet. At the root of all anger and hurt is an expectation or desire for the world or others to give us the peace that we can only find within ourselves through acceptance of what is.

Once we stop looking outside ourselves, practicing the magic of the soul becomes effortless and joyful. As you let go of the tendency to look outside yourself for your needs to be met, it will seem as if the world and everyone and everything in it is changing. All those people who created problems for you are now supporting you and can benefit from the peace you generate as a result of being needless. But is it that the world has changed or that you have changed? The answer is both. The outer world of form has changed for you because you have changed within.

You are the director
of the play that is your world.

SPIRITUAL MATURITY

We tend as humans to look (in the world of form) at how we are different from or better than others. This reflects an adolescent stage of human development. The developing child differentiates his or her views and behaviors from authority figures and challenges all convention in order to establish their own identity. This is healthy and necessary. Once that identity is achieved and developed into adulthood, the opportunity opens to recognize one's own values, appreciate the unique values of others, and sense the essential unity that lies at the core of all our values.

As a species, human beings are in spiritual adolescence (some might argue infancy). We still have a need to differentiate our self from others as a result of our yet immature mistaking of form for reality. Our perception in the world of form is that we are separate. In our spiritual adulthood—coming into our soul awareness—we recognize that we are both individual, human, and imperfect as well as one with all life, divine, and unlimited.

Anytime you notice that you are comparing yourself to someone else—that you are different or better in some way—practice noticing how you are alike. We are much more alike than we are different. We all have similar fears, hopes, dreams, hurts, and purposes. We are all striving for the same things—peace, fulfillment, a meaningful exis-tence. We can empower each other by recognizing our sameness and communicating our understanding of each other. We are connected on so many levels: physically through quantum energy, emotionally through our human weaknesses and our love, and spiritually through soul essence.

This has been a powerful and important lesson for me. Throughout my life, I have compared myself to others and judged others as a way of feeling better about myself. This is a common unconscious process for many of us designed to evade feelings of inadequacy or low self-esteem. When I practice seeing myself as one with everyone, it helps stretch my awareness beyond my own self-doubts and into a wider definition of self that empowers me as well as those around me.

What often stands in the way of recognizing our sameness is that when we are out of touch with our own weaknesses, we project them outward into the world and onto others. Anytime we judge others, we can look at ourselves and ask the question, "Is the behavior I am judging in this individual a quality that I dislike in myself?" Such introspection can open a door to a greater self-understanding. Our projections are an indirect way of creating a mirror for ourselves, so we can address our growth at deeper levels. Perhaps this process is orchestrated by the soul to provide us with a reflection to see ourselves more clearly when we are not willing to look into the mirror of self-examination ourselves. The friction that arises in relationships from such projections usually leads us to a more honest self-assessment. The key to healing and growth through such projections is acceptance. As we accept ourselves at the deepest levels, we automatically become accepting of others.

The more I recognize my connectedness with others on emotional and energetic (not just philosophical) levels, the more magical people I meet. I once heard a definition of enlightenment as "You know you are enlightened when you look out at the world and see the potential for enlightenment in everyone you meet." The next time you find yourself judging another, look into yourself and examine what you might not be accepting about yourself. Once you discover it, invoke the compassion of your soul for yourself and the one you were judging.

In facilitating classes that involved emotional release and healing, I have witnessed an interesting phenomenon that you have probably observed yourself in some fashion. An individual with an abrasive personality (or subpersonality) is seen in a different light after going through a cathartic experience, releasing and embracing a deep pain that is clearly the cause of their abrasiveness. The abrasiveness is a defense unconsciously designed to keep others from seeing their pain and, in most cases, to mask it from themselves as well. It will often manifest as a projection onto others. As others in the class experienced the catharsis and witnessed firsthand the profound vulnerability in the individual, their dislike for (or resistance to) him or her diminished or completely dissolved. Once we can clearly see someone else's pain and understand the cause of their behavior, our hearts open in compassion. We are in fact inspired to identify with their pain because it is very close in essence to our own. When we become vulnerable ourselves, or "soft of belly" as termed by spiritual writer Stephen Levine, we create rapport with others at the deepest emotional level. Some of my most intimate moments in life have been while sharing my deepest pains and fears with someone close to me.

Practice recognizing the essential sameness that you have with others. In doing so, you will likely experience the magic of your soul working not only to help you evolve but to help others evolve. From the perspective of soul, we are all one reflection of spirit seeking to grow. No one is better than anyone else. Jesus Christ and other great examples to humanity recognized their divine nature yet never indicated in any way that they were better than anyone else.

Humility is a word that describes the personality recognizing it is not superior. True humbleness is the experience of being one with all life, whether inanimate or alive (actually, all matter is alive!). True soul awareness recognizes the balance or inclusiveness between our divine greatness and the humbleness of our equality with everything that exists. If Jesus or the Buddha recognized that they were no better than you or me, how could we possibly think that we are any better than anyone else? Everyone is in a state of growing, and as we grow individually, we help to raise the quality of growth in all those with whom we are in relationship, at least to some degree.

The energy that is flowing through you, urging you to grow through your triumphs, failures, frustrations, and peak moments, is the same energy moving through the next person you meet after reading this passage. The person who pushes your frustration buttons shares that same magical energy that helps you to grow. The energy that you share is more truly who you both are than the two distinct (and possibly antagonistic) personalities that you perceive in the world of form. Look for that energy in everyone you see. Recognize that you are part of that energy. In Sanskrit, an ancient language designed specifically for describing spiritual reality, the word *Namaste* means, "I salute the divinity within you" or "the divinity within me salutes the divinity in you." Silently practice (or audibly if you have the nerve) greeting each person you meet during the day with an acknowledgement of their divinity. Many people in spiritual communities observe this practice or similar ones audibly throughout each day.

Practice radiating the light of your soul while you are with someone who is feeling down or sick. Don't say anything to try to make them feel better and notice how their mood changes as a result of being in your presence while you are in the presence of your soul. This is what effective spiritual teachers and really good, but rare therapists do. You can do it too.

Practice shifting your perspective of your identity from that of your individual self to that of being one with everyone. I know this may sound strange. You won't recognize the benefit from this exercise unless you try it. It is incredibly powerful. Practice extending your awareness to encompass your environment and everyone in it when you are standing in line at the bank, walking down the street, sitting at your desk, playing a sport, standing in a crowd of people, and so on. It is a simple thing to do when you think about it. The only difficulty might be remembering to think about it, but once you practice it on a regular basis, you may find that you enjoy the freedom and sense of power that can come from this exercise. You may recognize it as a refreshing break from being in your own head and thinking the thoughts with which you are normally identified. You may become enlightened beyond your wildest imagination. Try it just for fun or just to transform.

TAKING RESPONSIBILITY

We are taught in many ways to put our trust in powers outside ourselves. Many institutions try to control people by asserting (directly or subtly) that people need the institution. People can benefit from outside help, but all the power, every answer, all the peace is inside each individual. A helpful person or group is one who helps the individual recognize this truth. One of the advertisers in *Meditation* magazine was an organization called the Dispensable Church founded by Reverend Hugh Prather. I asked him once what the title meant. He said, "If a church truly does its job, it should make itself dispensable because people will grow beyond their need for a church." I found this to be a refreshing and unique perspective. Of course there are benefits to churches besides providing spiritual guidance, such as community, friendship, and service to others.

One way we can take back our power is to take responsibility for everything that happens to us. We sometimes avoid doing this because we don't want to feel guilty. We confuse responsibility with blame. Blame throws power outward and away from us. Responsibility draws power to us. Look for the ways that your actions and consciousness create your reality. It may not be that you are completely responsible for every single experience you have in your life, but there is always something that you can learn from every experience. By taking responsibility in all situations, you empower yourself toward greater growth. You can take responsibility even when something isn't completely in your control. Taking responsibility means giving yourself the power to change circumstances rather than being the victim of them.

Once you acknowledge your power, you can apply it to magic. We cannot realize the power to heal until we recognize our power to make ourselves sick. We cannot accept the power of a life of freedom until we admit it is our own beliefs that imprison us.

Shortly after I was promoted to managing editor at Sage Publications, I had an opportunity to take responsibility in a large way: Our most important journal at the time, *The Annals of the Academy of Social Sciences*, had printed with missing text. So, in my second month as managing editor, I had to communicate the issue to the president of the company, the owner of the company, the president of the board of *The Annals of the Academy of Social Sciences,* and a number of other high-profile people.

Now between you and me, there truly was nothing within reason that I could have done to prevent the incident. When the actual error occurred two months before, I had not yet been promoted and had no contact with that journal in my previous position. But I never mentioned any of that to the people with whom I had to communicate. I found out exactly how the error occurred, put a system in place to ensure it didn't happen again, and wrote a letter of apology with a plan to set the error right to the editor of the journal and the board members.

When I reported to the president about the issue, I took full responsibility for the error. I explained the new system that ensured it would never happen again and the plan to reprint the issue. When I walked out of the president's office, he was confident that the problem wouldn't happen again. I knew that if I had given him the plan and resolution but said there was nothing I could have done to avoid the problem, he would have had less confidence than if I had taken full responsibility for the problem.

Instead of being seen solely as having made a costly error in my first two months as managing editor, I was complimented and held in high regard for handling a critical situation with poise and competency. Any time you take responsibility for something that clearly is not "your fault," you increase your power and the confidence of those with whom you interact.

Look for the ways that you create your experiences in life and recognize that you can learn from each experience and that to a great degree you have the power to choose your reality.

Take responsibility and claim your power.

EMPOWERING OTHERS

Someone I once knew was awakened in the middle of the night by sounds in his living room downstairs. He described the event as follows:

As I walked out of my room, I knew that the sounds were from an intruder. I normally would have become frightened, but for some unknown reason, I slipped into an altered state of consciousness almost as though I didn't have a choice. I took a few steps down the stairs and saw a stranger quickly placing some of my most valuable possessions in a sack. The man looked up at me and hesitated, and I could see that he had a gun. In my heightened state, I chose my words thoughtfully. It felt as though someone were speaking through me. My words very simply were, "How can I help you?" Without a word, the man put down his sack and walked out of the house.

Rather than panicking and fearing for his life, he was somehow able to recognize that the man who was robbing him was in greater need than he was. He was able to rise above his own need for security and appreciate the pain in someone else. He said that he made a soul connection with the man in that moment. This is an extreme example of the magic of the soul—of what can happen when we transcend our own needs to empower others with soul power.

What does empowering others mean to you? What is your intent when you interact with others? How would your life be different if every interaction (or at least the majority) were dedicated to empowering others? Imagine how much less involved you would be in your own insecurity or pain. Seek balance in all things. You cannot truly empower others without empowering yourself as well. Do not sacrifice your needs for others—strive to give power to everyone and everything, including yourself.

Empowering others starts with the intention to do so. First try making it your goal to be a positive force in your interactions with others. If you would like to try a practical exercise for facilitating this, make a list with a heading on the left called negative and one on the right labeled positive. Place in the appropriate columns all thoughts, feelings, and behaviors that you might display during a day. Make a commitment to minimize the negative listings and emphasize the positive. Below is an example:

Negative	*Positive*
Discouraging thoughts	Positive attitude
Angry reactions	Encouraging others
Jealousy	Using humor
Gossiping	Listening well
Labeling others	Staying present
Judging others	Seeing the potential in others
Negative statements	Radiating light and love
Passive aggressiveness	Honesty

At a transpersonal level, empowering others means radiating light or soul energy through our thoughts, feelings, actions, and words. At a personal level, it can be as simple as offering encouragement rather than criticism, accepting someone instead of judging them, or choosing to recognize the positive in an individual instead of giving in to the urge to gossip about them. To take this a step further, imagine what it would be like to recognize the *divine energy* in everyone you meet throughout each and every day. Imagine acting with the understanding that God's life energy is flowing through everyone, and it is your job to help them recognize it through your interactions with them. Imagine how much power will flow through you with such an affirmation. Such a practice may be daunting for some people because it may seem idealistic. But is it really? Or can it also be practical? No one can really know until they try. I am certainly not perfect at this strategy, but the more I practice it the better I become. Each time I apply it, I reach a place of greater peace and power. We certainly have nothing to lose by allowing more love and appreciation for others to flow through us.

The first and most important place to apply this practice is with yourself, the second is in your home with those closest to you, and the third is in your business relationships. In one way, it is easier to apply it to those who are closest to you because you care more about them. In another way, it is more difficult because they are more involved in your growth process. They may push your buttons more, which again, is an indication that you are looking to them to fulfill your needs. This just presents a greater opportunity for a higher expression of your soul.

It can be a great challenge and a great opportunity to apply these principles with people who are less important in your life: people who create more work for you because of their inefficiency, the person who constantly bothers you with small talk, and the proverbial driver who cuts you off on the freeway. Why empower these people, you might ask? Why waste energy on people who cause you problems or are insignificant in your life?

Kahlil Gibran expressed it beautifully in *The Prophet*:

> You often say, "I would give, but only to the deserving."
> The trees in your orchard say not so, nor the flocks in your pasture.
> They give that they may live, for to withhold is to perish.
> Surely he who is worthy to receive his days and nights, is worthy of all else from you.
> And he who is deserved to drink from the ocean of life deserves to fill his cup from your little stream.[1]

In fact, when we give of the water of our little stream, it becomes one with the water of the ocean and the water of all life. When we reach out to another with love, our soul power and the power of God moves through us.

In varying degrees, every interaction either creates a greater expression of soul awareness or it creates the opposite. Every time we respond with empowerment toward others, we empower ourselves. The way we respond to the most frequent events (even though they may seem trivial) will determine the amount of soul contact that we make and share in our ongoing practice.

The following story, "Man with No Arms," was written by William Aldridge and published in *Meditation* magazine. It illustrates the potential magic in every moment, in every interaction we have with another. I have never read this story without tears appearing at its ending.

"Could you help me?" the stranger asked the man at the bus stop. Charlie looked up startled and suspicious, and squinted at the man through the late evening mist.

"Could you pull the hood from my face?" asked the stranger. "I have no arms."

"Sorry, fellow," Charlie said, happy to see the lighted bus coming down the street. "Sorry, but I am on my way to the hospital. I've a bad heart. I've got to be careful. Got a bad heart."

To the bus driver, Charlie said, "I should have lent him a hand. Simple thing. But he made me nervous. Dressed in a big black cape. Could barely see his eyes. Made my heart beat fast. And me on my way to the doctor's for my ulcer acting up." Charlie looked out of the bus window and saw the stranger stop in front of old Mrs. Reslap's place.

"Excuse me," said the stranger to the old woman. "Could you help me?"

Old Mrs. Reslap squinted at the stranger through her yellow eyes. "What kind of help you want?"

"Will you pull the hood from my face—I have no arms."

"I ain't spry like I used to be. You young people don't know what it's like, the least effort, after you reach seventy." She sat on her porch in the dim light of the street lamp and shouted across the yard to the stranger, "You had better go on down a bit, you'll find someone else to do your chore. Don't come bothering old ladies. You ain't that bad off."

"Thank you, anyway," said the stranger and walked on. At the corner, to the side of the church, he stopped in front of Reverend Casey, just stepping from his car.

"Excuse me, Reverend, could you help me? Will you pull the hood from my face? I have no arms."

"I certainly will," said the Reverend. "I'll be right with you. Just wait right here—or go inside while I put these papers in the safe."

For a long time, the stranger stood patiently in front of the church. From inside came sounds of community activity: "As president of Novco—and these gentlemen will go along with me,

Reverend—I feel it is imperative that you use your good offices to help us get Proposition Five passed . . ."

The stranger walked on and on, coming at last to the edge of town. Halfway across a high bridge, he stopped near a man looking down into the water. "Sir," he asked, "could you help me? Will you please pull the hood from my face. I have no arms."

"No," said the man. "I won't." He climbed over the railing and hung on, looking sadly down at the rush of wild water.

"Don't jump," pleaded the stranger. "I have no arms to assist you. You must help me. Pull the hood from my face."

The man jumped.

The stranger walked on across the bridge, his head bent forward. For several hours he climbed the steep hill on the opposite side. At last, nearing the top, he stood for a moment looking at the sleepy face of a little girl in the second-story window of a farmhouse.

She raised the sash and looked down at him. "Are you lost?" she asked.

"No," he answered. "But perhaps you can help me. Will you pull the hood from my face? I have no arms."

"I'm not supposed to go outside at night. But . . . if you feel bad—I'll come down. . . ."

At just that moment, an early morning wind blew through the treetops, across the meadow, around the house, and gently lifted the hood from the stranger's face. The face seemed to light up the entire mountain.

"Are you the sun?" asked the little girl.

"No," said the stranger. "I am love."[2]

Clearly, we experience love when we reach out to help others in any way. As it moves through us, we cannot help but be affected. We may not always know or understand the positive effects of each act of love that we offer. They may be far beyond what we can imagine. Remind yourself at the onset of every interaction with anyone or anything that this is an opportunity to become more filled with the light and love of your own soul. It is not crucial that you succeed in every instance. In fact, it is virtually impossible. But by reminding yourself, you create the awareness of the value of doing so. You can become the observer and watch how effective or ineffective you are. Through this process, you will grow so much more than going about daily interactions unconsciously.

Share the light of your soul.

Honesty is one of the most powerful ways to empower others. I make a practice of being honest about my feelings and observations with people who are receptive to my opinion. I don't normally offer my opinion if it is not welcome. If I sense, for example, that someone is sabotaging their prosperity as a result of a poverty consciousness, I will share my observation if I think it will help them recognize that they deserve prosperity. I will offer my compassion at the same time and perhaps cite an example of how I have recognized a similar dynamic within myself. If there is a chance that my feedback will help open a door, or at least point the way to it, I will take it and offer my understanding. Often a suggestion won't be received in the moment but will be realized at another point in time. It may sink in or another experience occurs and the question is already in the person's mind, "Am I recognizing that I deserve prosperity in this situation? Is there a way I can have a more empowering attitude?"

Being a manager was great training ground for learning the power of honesty. I have always been a sensitive person by nature, and as a result, I would often shy away from confronting others on their weaknesses. I soon realized that without honest feedback from manager to employee, people could not learn and grow. If I didn't provide honest feedback and benchmarks for improvement to employees, I might eventually have to fire them. By counseling employees, I discovered the power in honest feedback and applied it to other areas of my life. Much of my success as a corporate manager and director was the result of both positive and constructive feedback to employees, supervisors, and managers. It is also important to ask for feedback when offering it. When opening the channels of honesty is a two-way street, a greater potential for empowerment can be achieved. As I recognized the benefits of honest feedback to employees (as well as through other ongoing self-growth), I became less sensitive to constructive criticism myself. I became more accepting of my own weaknesses and wanted to learn and grow from feedback.

Protecting someone from our feelings or insights because we are afraid of hurting them is not compassionate. When we do this, we affirm that they are not strong enough to deal with whatever is challenging them. We empower when we believe that people are strong enough to handle whatever life hands them. Stuart Wilde, in his *Warrior's Wisdom* courses, shares a unique story. He was walking down the street in New York with some of his new age friends when a street person held out a cup for a contribution. Stewart reached into the cup, took a quarter, and said thank you. His friends were appalled at his lack of compassion. He explained to them that he was giving the homeless person an opportunity to see himself in another light. Rather than a beggar, he became a businessman who was affirming his wealth by offering money to strangers.

While I wouldn't go to such an extreme, the story does illustrate a comical if not outrageous example of empowering people by affirming their strength. If your motive for helping others is because they are not strong enough to help themselves, it may be more an act of codependence than one of compassion. More consistent with the magic of your soul is to help others from the sheer joy of the experience. If you feel you are sacrificing by giving, then you aren't truly giving. Surrender to the gift. Recognize that the gift, the giver, and the receiver are all part of the same energy. When you give to someone else, you are giving to yourself. When you receive, you are giving too. This is true whether we are talking about giving feedback, material gifts, love, or the magic of our soul.

I recently developed a system for applying honest feedback to myself based on the performance review system that served me so well in management. I used an annual written review and six months later, a formal verbal review to assess employee performance. Any efficient manager knows the importance of creating specific goals, providing guidance in achieving them, and offering feedback assessing progress along the way. I applied this strategy to my own spiritual growth and performance in empowering others by writing a job description (presented below) and giving myself consistent feedback and annual written reviews indicating my progress, areas for improvement, and goals for the future.

Spiritual Job Description
Qualifications
Must be kind, forgiving, flexible, understanding, mindful, self-loving, compassionate, open, powerful, and possess integrity, honesty, and consistent contact with spiritual energy.
Main Duties
Spread light everywhere
Offer kindness to all
Go beyond self-interest
Offer healing to those who ask for it
Be understanding when others are unreasonable
Focus will toward good
Empower others at all times
Remain humble
Breathe deeply and live in ecstasy
Recognize magic in every moment
Be present and nurturing to pain in others
Be present and nurturing to myself
Forgive self when failing at above duties
Accept self completely while striving to be the best human I can be
Other Duties
Write books, articles, and Web content
Maintain spiritual dialogue through Web site
Teach through lectures, workshops, and media appearances
Perform weddings and other spiritual ceremonies
Provide counseling and healing services

If you are serious about your spiritual growth and how you influence those around you, I highly recommend this exercise. Ideally, every week or at least every month, take out your self-described spiritual job description and give yourself feedback on how you are doing and how you can improve. This method can be fun and extremely effective. At least once a year, give yourself a written review praising your accomplishments, indicating areas for continued improvement and listing specific goals to achieve in the coming year.

Another excellent way of empowering others is to let them empower you. Children often ask for guidance from adults. But have you ever noticed how they light up when they teach *you* something? In your quest to be a positive force in the world, be sure that you are receiving light as well as radiating it.

Empowering others automatically brings light into our lives because we are consciously seeking to share more light. This light not only moves into the areas we direct it outwardly, but it also provides more light for our own growth. When we support the growth of others, we greatly enhance our own growth and our ability to create fulfillment for ourselves and those we influence. We never learn anything more fully than when we teach it. The more we support others, the more the universe supports us. When we share spirit with others, we become spirit.

Joy is the gift you receive
when the smiles you create on
the faces of others shine back on you.

PLANETARY AWAKENING

Each person who strives to become a light in the world makes it easier for the next. We are at a point on our planet where more and more people are awakening. The surge of information about and instructing toward spiritual awareness is amazing. According to *Publishers Weekly*, spirituality has been the fastest growing literature genre for five straight years.

Another example of the increase in interest toward spirituality is the continuing success of the *Oprah Winfrey Show*. The show has been the number one syndicated daytime talk show for almost all of the time it has been broadcasting. In 1998, Oprah changed the format to include a more directly spiritual focus and called it "Change Your Life TV." It included a segment called "Remembering your Spirit." The new format was designed to inspire viewers to fulfill their own dreams by understanding themselves better through self-exploration, emotional healing, and meditation. After several years, the show has remained in the number one spot. This huge daytime television audience consists of people self-actualizing, healing, and making a difference in the world as a result of Oprah's bold decision to increase the expression of the light of her soul through her work.

Each person who learns how to create a positive field of energy influences everyone they contact toward the same ability. Each person who communicates that ability to others adds to the collective thought pool of a humanity striving toward spiritual evolution.

You may have already heard of the hundredth monkey syndrome, outlined in *The Hundredth Monkey* by Ken Keyes Jr.[3] An experiment began in 1952 with scientists providing sweet potatoes to monkeys on the island of Koshima. One monkey got the notion that the sweet potatoes would be more palatable if they didn't have sand on them, so this eighteen-month-old female monkey began washing her potatoes in a nearby stream before eating them. Under the observation of the scientists, she taught this innovation to her mother and her playmates. Soon, other monkeys started to model the behavior. The increase in the number of monkeys who learned the process was gradual until 1958 when the amount of monkeys reached a *critical mass*. Suddenly, almost all of the monkeys started washing their potatoes. But the most amazing result was that at that same time, colonies of monkeys on neighboring islands also started washing potatoes without having gone through the modeling process that occurred on the first island. This suggested that once enough members of a species learn a given behavior, it becomes part of the social unconscious of that species and therefore part of the instinctual process.

Rupert Sheldrake, the renowned biochemist and author of *The Rebirth of Nature*, explains how this phenomenon occurs in his theory of morphic resonance in an article in *Meditation* magazine. "Each organism has within and around it an energetic field, and each field is connected to every other morphic field through morphic resonance."[4] In other words, we are all connected, which seekers of spiritual awareness have been discovering on an experiential level for eons. So anything we do or think affects others through our morphic resonance. The more individuals who think or behave in similar ways, the more they influence others in a particular species. This is true whether it is a positive or negative influence. With this knowledge, the motivation to think in positive, healthy ways becomes enhanced as we recognize how we affect everyone else on the planet.

The availability of information in our technological society increases this process exponentially. The internet—which Marilyn Ferguson, the renowned brain researcher and author of the landmark book *The Aquarian Conspiracy*, has called the nervous system of the planet—allows people to communicate their thoughts and inspirations around the world in seconds. We can know almost instantly how people on the other side of the world are reacting to a world situation. Imagine how much further we will evolve as a species if and when we can all speak one language or have technology that will translate instantaneously. Imagine a world where everyone can understand everyone else and communication is immediate. Would wars continue if everyone in the attacked country could contact everyone in the attacking country, thereby connecting the reaction of violence from heart to heart instantaneously?

In some ways it is easier for someone to reach enlightenment today than it was 2,000 years ago or even 100 years ago. It is easier to evolve in consciousness today than it was yesterday because more people have evolved in the last twenty-four hours. It makes the accomplishments of Christ, the Buddha, Mohammed, or Lao Tsu that much more astonishing to realize that they achieved such advanced states with far fewer models or tools. Jesus didn't have the Bible to help him evolve. There was no Tao Te Ching for Lao Tsu to contemplate.

We live in such an exciting time. Each one of us has an unparalleled opportunity to contribute to our evolving planet. Even though the energy of the collective unconscious increasingly supports this truth, the answer is not *out there*. It is within each one of us. The love from your soul is the most powerful magical elixir. Each time you open to it, it expands your awareness to embrace your oneness with all. The more people, things, and consciousness that your desire and prayers seek to fulfill, the more powerful will be your magic. The more evolved we become, the more surely will be our mission to serve all that is. The more expansive our desire, the more evolved the level of spirit is that we invoke to fulfill our magic.

You are the light of the world.

I recommend meditating or praying daily to focus your soul light into the world. The following exercise is a magical formula for setting the tone for your day or accomplishing any goal. I have used it to manifest goals or whenever I prepare for an important meeting, present a speech, perform a wedding, or set my intention to empower others throughout the day. After doing the exercise, I know that I have already created the effect for which I am aiming, and all I have to do in the performance of the act is surrender to my guidance and to the energy that has already been created through the ritual.

This process mirrors the natural progression of any creation into reality. Every creative manifestation begins as an idea in thought or an image, is empowered by enthusiastic emotion, and is galvanized by the physical energy of action. Once these have been accomplished, the magic is done and the idea has no choice but to manifest in some form. The quality of the form will be determined by the quality of intent, desire, and intelligent action behind its manifestation.

❊   ❊   ❊

Exercise for Creating Magic
(Track 5 on Audio CD)

Visualize the day ahead of you. Imagine yourself going about your daily activities. What qualities would you like to be present in your activities? Love? Compassion? Trust? Skill? Integrity? Power? Light? Competence? Caring? Humor? Whatever qualities you decide, see them manifested on the faces of those you encounter. Through your imagery, it has already been achieved in mind.

Feel those same qualities in your heart as well as in the hearts of others you encounter. It has already been achieved in feeling.

What colors would these qualities be if you viewed them as energy? Red? Yellow? Rose? Green? Violet? Orange? Blue? Chartreuse? Teal? Amethyst? Turquoise? See the appropriate colors as part of the scene. It has already been achieved in energetic form.

Ask the spiritual forces that guide you to help manifest your intent on the physical plane. Feel the energy and see it as light pouring in through the top of your head and moving out of the front of your body into the thought form you are creating. It has been accomplished.

Give thanks for the day that you have made real and know that its accomplishment in the world of perception is now just a formality as it takes form in space and time.

❊   ❊   ❊

4

God

There is so much religious debate about who or what God is. The funny thing is that everyone is right. God is everything. Every interpretation of God is correct, because God exists in every way that God is conceivable. In Hinduism, it is common to worship hundreds of different gods but with the understanding that they are all different aspects of one God. The greater our ability to experience God, the more unified our understanding becomes.

My understanding of God has grown in proportion to my own spiritual evolution. One of my early teachers, the late Dr. Earl D. Barnum, once asked, "How is your concept of God different today than your concept of God when you were seven years old? Did God change or did your understanding grow?" It becomes more and more clear to me and others who go deeper into their faith or practice that there is only one God with many different faces. God in His/Her greatness is so far beyond what the human mind can conceive, that each individual is capable of only an infinitesimal degree of understanding of the totality of Infinite Divinity. If we use a diamond as a symbol of God, we can recognize that what each individual (and each particular faith) sees as the one God is just one facet of the diamond. There is a richness that goes deep into the diamond that is glimpsed by those who are fortunate enough to *experience* God.

I refer to God as both masculine and feminine because that is how I experience Him/Her. But this also makes sense on an intellectual level. If God is Creator—or in my own terms, the Creative Principle—then it is only logical that He/She possesses both feminine and masculine energy. Neither can create independent of the other.

The more I grow spiritually, the wider becomes my understanding and description of God. Surprisingly, I now find myself feeling akin to people who are at both extremes of the religious spectrum: atheists and those of traditional religious conviction. Clearly, my philosophical views are not traditional, but I find a commonality in the expression of God with those who are devout in their faith regardless of what religion to which they ascribe. When Jehovah's Witnesses come to my door, we have delightful conversations about applying spirit in life from which I learn new understandings. At a time when I was trying to prove my beliefs to myself, I found it enjoyable to debate with religious fundamentalists (also frustrating because no one ever wins such debates). Now I find it much more enjoyable and enriching to look for the points where we agree, the points through which we can support each other.

On the other end of the spectrum, I find my views in close alignment with those who consider themselves atheists. My personal definition of God is a Creative Principle that runs through all life. Those who consider themselves atheists will generally agree that such a principle exists; they just don't call it God. The major difference between our understanding then is that I call this Principle God because I want to acknowledge the sacredness I experience in Him/Her. There is a value in acknowledging this sacredness. The more we honor anything in life, the closer our relationship becomes to that person, place, thing, or principle. The more we honor God, or the Creative Principle, the more we become immersed in His/Her power and love. Another difference between my understanding and that of an atheist is that I believe and experience God as self-knowing or self-conscious but it is a consciousness that is beyond what the human mind can grasp.

We tend to give God human characteristics because humanity is the highest form of life we experience with our senses. Each culture ascribes to God the characteristics that are found in that culture, and each individualized understanding generally conforms to the values of the individual. In other words, *we* create God in our own image. I have read no finer treatise on the subject of stages of God realization than the explanation in *How to Know God* by Deepak Chopra. In addition to explaining the different descriptions of God based on the spiritual evolution of the individual doing the interpreting, his book offers an inspirational motivation for the reader to evolve toward higher levels of God awareness.

EXPERIENCING GOD

We begin to transcend attributing human characteristics to God when we begin to *experience* God beyond a mental understanding. So how do we experience God? The most dependable way I know is through transcending the mind in meditation. Prayer is talking to God and meditation is listening or, more fully, experiencing God. When we still the mind, we cannot help but experience God, because God is everywhere present beneath the surface of sensory perception.

It really can be quite simple once we let go of even a minimal degree of the control of our mind. Our mind is what holds together our view of the world. It creates a practical order to an energetic reality that we are not ready to experience fully. So, the mind and its rationality are helpful and necessary functions. But because the human mind is still infantile in its development (compared to organic life, for example), it is undisciplined and operates in a controlling manner. Like a young child, the mind places its demands on its environment, believing that it is the center of attention and the most important part of reality.

By quieting the mind with practice, we are pulled into the experience of God. By disciplining and using it in a more functional way—to rise above analysis to higher realms—we open to a reality that can only be experienced by surrendering to a higher order. Often when I meditate and succeed at bringing the mind to a point of rest, I find tears forming and rolling down my face as I am overtaken by the profound beauty of the energy of God that is exposed in the silence. It is an energy so loving that it goes beyond any definition of love that can be communicated. It is so profound that it cannot be adequately described. I experience its quality as a simple support-iveness of all life—a beautiful, soft, nurturing presence that cares for every form of life everywhere.

The great mystics and saints of all ages have reported experi-ences of oneness with God. But many otherwise average individuals have been blessed with such extraordinary experiences as well. *The Imprisoned Splendor*, by Raynord C. Johnson, contains a number of inspiring accounts of cosmic or God consciousness listed from many different sources.[1] Many of these accounts were not preceded by any particularly reverent circumstances, but all of them required (or per-haps inspired) a suspension of the normal rational process. Below are four examples from sources listed in *The Imprisoned Splendor* that I include here to inspire and point to the experience to which the magic of the soul can lead us.

From *The Psychic Sense:*

> I was sitting on the seashore, half-listening to a friend arguing violently about a matter which merely bored me. Unconsciously to myself, I looked at a film of sand I had picked up on my hand, when I suddenly saw the exquisite beauty of every little grain of it: instead of being dull, I saw that each particle was made up of a per-fect geometrical pattern, with sharp angles, from each of which a brilliant shaft of light was reflected, while each tiny crystal shone like a rainbow. The rays crossed and recrossed, making exquisite patterns, of such beauty that they left me breathless.

> I was used, at odd intervals to seeing the invisible counterpart of minute objects, but this was quite unexpected and fascinating. Then, suddenly, my consciousness was lighted up from within and I saw in a vivid way how the whole universe was made up of par-ticles of material which, no matter how dull and lifeless they might seem at first sight, were nevertheless filled with this intense and vital beauty.

> For a second or two, the whole world appeared as a blaze of glory. When it died down, it left with me something I have never forgotten and which constantly reminds me of the beauty locked up in every minute speck of material around me.[2]

From *The Story of My Heart:*

I was not more than eighteen when an inner and esoteric meaning began to come to me from all the visible universe, and indefinable aspirations filled me. I found them in the grassy fields, under the trees, on the hilltops, at sunrise, and in the night. There was a deeper meaning everywhere. The sun burned with it; a deep feeling entered me while gazing at the sky in the azure noon, and in the star-lit evening.

I was sensitive to all things, to the earth under, and the star-hollow round about; to the least blade of grass, to the largest oak. They seemed like exterior nerves and veins for the conveyance of feeling to me. Sometimes a very ecstasy of exquisite enjoyment of the entire visible universe filled me.[3]

The passage below was the experience of The Blessed Angelico of Foigno, a Christian mystic of the thirteenth century.

All that I beheld was the ineffable fullness of God; but I can relate nothing of it, save that I have seen the fullness of Divine Wisdom, wherein is all goodness. . . .

All that I say of this, seems to me to be nothing. I feel as though I offend in speaking of it, for so greatly does the Good exceed all my words that my speech seems to be but blasphemy. . . .

The eyes of my soul were opened and I beheld the plenitude of God, by which I understood the whole world both here and beyond the sea, the abyss, and all other things. . . . And in this I beheld nothing save the Divine Power, in a way that is utterly inde-scribable, as that through the greatness of its wonder the soul cried with a loud voice saying, "The whole world is of God." Wherefore I understood that the world is but a little thing; and I saw that the power of God was above all things and the whole world was filled with it. . . .

And finally, from *Contemplations:* The person experiencing this event had no previous mystical episodes. He was in a church and observed an expanding luminous violet haze coming through the stones in the aisle at his side.

Upon the instant the luminous blue haze engulfing me and all around me became transformed into golden glory, into light untellable. . . . The golden light of which the violet haze seemed now to have been as the veil or outer fringe, welled forth from a central immense globe of brilliancy. . . . But the most wonderful thing was that these shafts and waves of light, that vast expanse of photosphere, and even the great central globe itself, were crowded to solidarity with the forms of living creatures . . . a single coherent organism filling all space and place, yet composed of an infinitude of individuated existences . . . I saw moreover that these beings were present in teeming myriads in the church I stood in; that they were intermingled with and were passing unobstructedly through both myself and all my fellow-worshipers. . . . The heavenly hosts drifted through the human congregation as wind passes through a grove of trees; beings of radiant beauty and clothed in shimmering raiment. . . .

But this vast spectacle of mingled heaven and earth was succeeded by an even richer experience; one in which everything of time and place and form vanished from my consciousness and only the ineffable eternal things remained. . . . And as the point of a candle-flame leaps upward when an object is held just above it, so the flame of my consciousness leapt to its utmost limit and passed into the region of the formless and uncreated to tell of which all words fail. . . .[4]

To someone who has never experienced such a phenomenon, these accounts may seem extraordinary, unbelievable, but hundreds of thousands, maybe even millions have had them. There are so many sources that profess similar experiences of oneness. How many more people never communicated them at the risk of being labeled insane? But experiencing God does not have to consist of a supernatural state. It can be a simple inner peace or a feeling of love for everyone and everything. How many billions have had this experience at some time or another throughout the course of history? The goal is simply to expand the experience, to make it real in our lives on a more consistent basis.

Try this now—close your eyes (after reading this paragraph) and recognize that you don't have to think. The mind is so persistently (even obsessively) active. Allow your mind to simply take a break from its constant movement. Try watching your breath. Try imagining light moving through you. Feel your heart opening wide and the love within you expanding outward. Try just letting go completely and finding what is there beneath your self-identification, beneath your mental hold on reality. You can do it. Some people experience fear because of the natural instinct of self-preservation. When the mind stops, it can feel like the self is dying. In a sense it is. The illusory, separate self is dying for a moment to give way to a more expansive, truer reality that cannot be contained by the mind or any part of the personality. By letting go of your sense of individual self, you will lose nothing and very literally gain everything. In fact, you will become everything.

Be one with God.

If you experience the energy the way I do, you will feel a tingling sensation in and around your body. Try identifying with the tingling. That is the energy of God you are feeling even if it is just a minute, fractional expression of God's energy. If you get really good at this, which may take practice or may happen instantly, you will start to realize that you are the energy (the tingling) moving through and around your body as well as through all life. You will recognize that you are part of, or more precisely, are one with the God energy that connects all life. We can move beyond even the experience of God because if the individual "I" is experiencing it, we are still identified with "I" as separate. We can become one with God without separation, because after all, this is who we really are. When I interviewed Pir Vilayat Inayat Khan, the western head of the Sufi Order, he put it this way: "Everything can be seen from the Divine vantage point, in which we are the object of the Divine knowledge rather than thinking of God as an object of our knowledge. That shifting vantage point triggers off ecstasy."[5]

At any moment you are in touch with this ecstasy, you will find it difficult to hurt or even disregard any manifestation of God in form because it is part of you. This is why many eastern sects practice vegetarianism and are against killing even an insect.

It's kind of funny that I would write "even an insect" as though an insect is less significant because of its size. Many people are outraged at those who would wear an animal that was killed for its skin and, at the same time, would think nothing of wiping out an entire civilization of ants marching across their patio. Is there any less consciousness in an ant than there is in a mink? Actually, ants are a relatively advanced species, but judging the value of a being by its intelligence is also invalid when we recognize God in everything. I do not mean to expound a moral conviction about vegetarianism or abstaining from killing insects. I am not a vegetarian (although I have practiced at different times in my life). I do practice honoring every form of life and recognizing the sacredness of every animal or plant (plants have feelings and God life as well) that is sacrificed to give me nourishment. There are times when we may find it necessary to kill insects as part of common sense health practices (I am sure there are valid moral arguments against this, however). But the point is that everything has God's energy moving through it and is no less important because it doesn't have a human mind. When we are in the experience of that God consciousness, we are inspired to support all life, all of creation.

Try experiencing that tingling in different settings. Try being the light when you are with other people or doing your job or driving your car. Experience the bliss of expanded awareness as often as you can.

THE INFINITUDE OF GOD

God exists on every level imaginable. God is transcendent. He/She exists as a being that is greater than all of His/Her parts because He/She is the sum total of all that exists. God is also immanent. He/She exists within every cell of every being. Each cell is a universe that contains infinite particles of God. Every universe is but a cell in the body and soul of God. There are levels of Godness or divine purpose like circles within circles moving outward through infinite existence.

When praying to God,
try praying to the God
in your heart as well as
the God of infinite reality.

Just as a hologram holds the completed structure in each of its smallest parts, a single cell in your heart holds the complete structure of God. That cell is also a microcosm of the divine nature and divine purpose within your entire body, your consciousness, your soul. Your identity is a part of the divine purpose that is the soul of your family, your community, and all your relationships. We are all part of the divine purpose that lives within the soul of our country. This country, just like your family and community, has a divine purpose that is linked to the purpose of our planet. Our planet is a cell in the body of the solar system, which also has a divine purpose and identity. The solar system is a cell in the consciousness of the universe, which is a cell in the body of Infinite Universes. Each level of divine purpose is a higher or more evolved expression of God and awareness.

We evolve as our identification of our self expands to include these various levels. As humans, our divine heritage is to expand our self-awareness to include our family, our groups, our humanity, our planet, and everything that is. The soul is not isolated. When we are centered in the magic of the soul, we are aware of ourselves as part of the soul of our planet and as part of all that is. Mata Amritanandamayi, who is recognized as one of India's living saints, received the Divine Mother at about age ten. She later said that since that day "nothing could be seen as different from my own formless Self wherein the entire universe exists as a tiny bubble."

This is one reason spiritually focused people are moved to help others and to live in balance with the nature of the planet and the natural laws of the universe. Since we are all one beyond the level of the physical plane, we help ourselves when we assist others. We assist others when we help ourselves. At the level of soul, I am you and you are me. We are one in eternity.

In the Old Testament, God proclaims to Moses, "I am That I am." I—the consciousness speaking through the burning bush—am all that is. You are that "I am" also. You are God expressing through human form. You are part of Infinite Reality. Recognize your oneness with God—with everything that exists in every possible way. Repeat the affirmation:

I am That I am.

If God is everything, then God is you and you are God. You are human, imperfect, evolving and, at the same time, a perfect and divine soul. What a splendid dichotomy. The practice of the magic of the soul and all spiritual practices is to deepen one's experience of God or the Creative Principle that flows through all life.

☀ ☀ ☀

Exercise on Expansion

For free audio version, http://www.livingpurposeinstitute.com/meditation.htm

Close your eyes and be aware of your body. Imagine that you are a single cell in your body and, as that cell, a divine spark of light. You contain within you a divine purpose—a purpose toward health, toward promoting life on all levels. Imagine that you are a cell in your heart with a

purpose of loving. Imagine that you are all the cells in your body working in perfect harmony to sustain health and to promote your purpose for living. Imagine you are the soul of each cell in your body that makes up the soul of you. . . .

What is your purpose?
Imagine you are the soul of your family. . . .
What is your purpose?
Imagine you are the soul of your country. . . .
What is your purpose?
Imagine you are the soul of the planet. . . .
What is your purpose?
Imagine you are the soul of the solar system. . . .
What is your purpose?
Imagine you are the soul of infinite reality. . . .
What is your purpose?

❋   ❋   ❋

THE UNIVERSALITY OF GOD

I once attended a spiritual event headed by Pir Vilayat Inayat Khan, the western leader of Sufism, which is a mystical branch of Islam that promotes unity of spiritual people and faiths. The event consisted of a panel of clergy from different religions, including a Buddhist monk, Christian minister, Hindu priest, Zoroastrian priestess, and Jewish rabbi. Each one had been invited to speak about the meaning of light from their respective traditions. The interesting outcome was that each speaker was in complete agreement with the thoughts of every other speaker. The summary of the collective agreement was that light is the expression of God's reflection that moves through all creation.

The rabbi spoke last. He spoke with an awe-inspired voice as he said from his heart, "I was very skeptical about participating in such an ecumenical function, as I am not a liberal rabbi. I did not imagine there could be a meeting of minds in such an arena as this. But I am confounded because after hearing everyone else's comments, I have nothing to say. It has all been said. Everything spoken is consistent with our understanding of light in Judaism."

With that he broke into a beautifully melodic song in Hebrew about light. After the discussion, a wedding and baptism took place that was scheduled to be performed by the minister. Pir Vilayat gathered all the clergy and blessed the bride and groom and later all participated in the baptism. I have sometimes wondered what became of the couple and the baby that were blessed by the distinguished spiritual leaders. Imagine the spiritual power that is actualized when true leaders of spiritual faiths and disciplines come together in unified service of God's light. Imagine the power of all people of all faiths coming together to pray or meditate for good in the world. This is one of my dreams and is the dream of many who seek to go beyond their individual understanding of spirit to embrace a larger community of spiritual understanding, a community that is already integrated and working together at the level of soul.

Swami Satchidananda is a highly respected Hindu spiritual teacher and ecumenical advocate. When I interviewed him for an article titled "Many Roads Home" in *Meditation* magazine, he recounted an experience while at the Vatican. He was questioned by a cardinal. "How can there be many paths to one goal, God?" Swamiji, as he is respectfully called by his friends, responded, "Sir, you are living in Rome, you should not be asking me this question. *All roads lead to Rome*. If Rome itself can have so many roads, why would we think our *home* will have only one road?"[6]

I believe we are at a point in our development when many people are inspired by such a dream as people coming together in spiritual service regardless of religious persuasion. As a minister who performs many nondenominational or mixed-denominational marriages, I have received a strong interest and agreement from couples about the idea of embracing the truth at the heart of all religions. In order to embrace such an ideal, we must be willing to see beyond religious forms. At a higher level, we can recognize that the power and love of God manifest within and through different practices in different ways. At the level of spiritual practice—which comes from the heart—it is easy to find a common ground that can bring us together. Every religion has a similar code of ethics. It is at the level of belief—which comes from the mind—that we find polarity and conflict. With polarity and conflict rampant, what our world needs most is for people to relate more consistently from the heart.

At the level of archetypes, religious beliefs are not in conflict. A world where spiritual leaders and practitioners of all types work together in united prayer and practice for the common good is the dynamic that occurs from the sphere of the soul. Imagine the power of adding conscious participation from the personalities and organizations representing the soul's influence on earth.

The tragedy of the September 11, 2001, attack on the World Trade Center and ensuing world conditions compelled many Americans to study the teachings of Islam. The understanding that has resulted for those who truly wanted to learn is a realization that different faiths have much more in common than they have in conflict. At the core of all spiritual thought is a message of kindness, justice, love, compassion, trust, understanding, and faith. Just as the one soul manifests itself through the many personalities in the world of form, so too are various religions individual expressions of the one truth.

Another sign that the world is ready to move in a direction toward increased appreciation for the spiritual forms of others happened a few weeks before writing this passage. I attended the baptism of my friend's three children. She is Catholic but was not married in the church so she had a hard time finding a priest who would baptize them. She finally found a small Greek Orthodox Church that would perform the ceremony. The service was done in Spanish (and some English), which is my friend's first language.

The church was modest in appearance. It was basically a room with twelve pews, a tree growing through the floor and the ceiling, and a few religious statues and pictures. And . . . it had a brilliant sense of spirit. Before Father Juan Correa began the ceremony, he briefly explained the difference between Greek Orthodox and Roman Catholic practices and philosophy and asked if there were any questions. I asked him, "How do you experience God?" At first, he began to explain the Greek Orthodox concept of God. Then I clarified by saying, "I really meant, how do you experience God personally?"

His essential response in broken English (but eloquent in body language and energy) was, "God is a light that moves through me in everything that I do and everyone I touch."

I smiled, inspired by his wisdom and then commented that "I was raised Catholic and was taught that if people weren't baptized before they died, they would not go to heaven."

"We are in a new millennium now," he responded. "We now believe that it doesn't matter if you are baptized; it is a matter of what you do in life. I also do not believe in a fiery hell as a punishment for sins."

"And what is heaven?" I asked. "Is it a place where we go or is it a state of consciousness?"

His answer gave me chills. "Heaven is what [the experience] we create through the good things we do in life."

This experience was a symbol to me that people in all faiths are waking up to the *experience* of God—a symbol that was provided to me while writing this book to inspire in others this understanding.

Most people you ask will agree that there is a distinction between religion and spirituality. Religion is the organized worship of God or some higher principle. Spirituality, in my definition, is the practice of spiritual principles. What makes a religion spiritual is the spiritual practice of those who are members of a religion or spiritual community.

In my experience, the more organized a religion is or, more specifically, the more dogma that is handed down through a hierarchy the more difficult it is to experience its spirituality. Any system that asks its followers to accept a doctrine without questioning it with their own experience is asking people to cut their connection with their soul. Blind faith is accepting a particular belief without questioning. Spiritually empowered faith is trusting that there is a higher or divine purpose for every event life offers even if we can't see it in the moment. If we can't understand why a particular event has occurred in our lives, trusting that there is a higher and divine order is an act of faith. But the more we experience God the less we require faith, because we become one with the creative energy of God. We can see that every event is an act of creation even if it is one that challenges our comfort or safety at the level of form.

If you are involved in a religious organization, you can infuse it with spirituality by utilizing it as a means for expressing your soul and your experience of truth. The greatest advantage to being in a spiritual community is the community. We grow in our spiritual awareness through interaction with and mutual support of those who share a common spiritual practice.

You do not necessarily need an organized approach to grow spiritually. Every tree I have ever met has had as much spiritual energy as any statue I have ever experienced. I can feel God more clearly in nature than in a building, but that is a personal preference.

I have also experienced profound spirit in the midst of spiritual ceremonies in many different traditional settings. We can bring our own sense of spirit or soul energy to every religious setting (or any experience at all). I have meditated and chanted with Buddhists. I have participated in Hindu ceremonies. I have prayed and sang in 120° heat in the darkness of the Native American sweat lodge ceremony. I have chanted with the Hare Krishna. I have prayed with almost every Christian denomination. I have performed wedding ceremonies in concert with rabbis and participated in Jewish rituals. I have joined in, promoted, and presented ceremonies that included prayers and chanting from all different faiths in one place and time. I have interviewed and had intimate conversations with leaders from all different paths of spiritual pursuit and found that beneath it all is the one profound experience that we call God.

I experience the presence of God in my deepest meditations and my most profound moments as a supportive, creative intelligence that pervades all life. These words only describe a muted, fractional representation of the feeling. It is supreme joy in just being. This light that runs through all life is likened to love, but even the word love is inadequate. The love we speak of in our language can be withheld or blocked. The love of eternal light cannot be blocked or contained. It just is. It is a force so strong that it keeps life alive. It sustains energy in infinite existence.

The energy of God is impersonal because it transcends personality. When it flows through us, however, it becomes personal. The magic of being human is that when we receive and radiate God's energy, it becomes love as it moves through us, the most perfect, pure form of love—completely unconditional. When we are filled with the love of God, we cannot help but give love through all that we do, to everyone and everything we contact. The energy of God is relentless.

Receive the energy of God, and
your love will be relentless.

I was once walking along a mountain ridge looking down at the San Fernando Valley in California, where I was born and raised. It had once been filled with fruit orchards. Over the years, a city had sprung up filling the area with more and more buildings and more concrete to make it easier to get from one building to another. But as I walked along the mountain range, there were still more trees to be seen than buildings, more green than gray. I realized that no matter how powerful mankind thinks it is, it cannot kill nature. If we disappeared from this planet, it would only a be matter of time before all of the structures and monuments of modern technology and industrialization would deteriorate and give way to new nature. As soon as a small crack occurs in pavement, nature will be springing up looking for life.

I was once inspired while sitting alone at the top of a waterfall in the mountains. A pine tree grew out of the side of a solid rock wall. Its trunk protruded from a crack in the rock and bent upward reaching toward the sun as a testimony to the power and persistence of life.

I am always impressed by the profound humility in Native American tradition. There is such an appreciation of the sacredness of nature. God is not seen as a distant ruler but a spirit that infuses all life. There are the Great Grandfather and the Great Grandmother, which are representatives of God transcendent, but there is also the appreciation for those forces as they are manifested in all of creation as God immanent. In 1854, Chief Seattle responded to the offer from the United States government to buy land from the Native Americans and "reserve" them a place to live. His response has been called one the most compelling pieces ever written about preserving the environment but also illustrates the connection between God and nature and the sad loss that has occurred through the industrialization of this continent. Below is an abbreviated version of Chief Seattle's response.

> How can you buy or sell the sky, the warmth of the land? The idea is strange to us. If we do not own the freshness of the air and the sparkle of the water, how can we buy them?
>
> Every part of the earth is sacred to my people. Every shining pine needle, every sandy shore, every mist in the dark woods, every clearing and humming insect is holy in the memory and experience of my people. The sap, which courses through the trees, carries the memories of the red man. The white man's dead forget the country of their birth when they go to walk among the stars. Our dead never forgot this beautiful earth for it is the mother of the red man. We are part of the earth and it is part of us. The perfumed flowers are our sisters; the deer, the horse, the great eagle, these are our brothers. The rocky crests, the juices in the meadows, the body heat of the pony, and man—all belong to the same family.
>
> So, when the Great Chief in Washington sends word that he wishes to buy our land, he asks much of us. The Great Chief sends

word he will reserve us a place so that we can live comfortably to ourselves. He will be our father and we will be his children. So we will consider your offer to buy our land. But it will not be easy. For this land is sacred to us. The shining water that moves in the streams and rivers is not just water but the blood of our ancestors. If we sell our land, you must remember that it is sacred, and you must teach your children that it is sacred and that each ghostly reflection in the clear water in the lakes tells of events and memories in the life of my people. The water's murmur is the voice of my father's father. The rivers are our brothers, they quench our thirst. The rivers carry our canoes, and feed our children.

The air is precious to the red man, for all things share the same breath—the beast, the tree, the man, they all share the same breath. The white man does not seem to notice the air he breathes. But if we sell you our land, you must remember that the air is precious to us, that the air shares its spirit with all the life it supports. The wind that gave our grandfather his first breath also receives his last sigh.

And if we sell you our land, you must keep it apart and sacred, as a place where even the white man can go to taste the wind that is sweetened by the meadow's flowers. So we will consider your offer to buy our land. If we decide to accept, I will make one condition: The white man must treat the beast of this land as his brothers. I am a savage and I do not understand any other way. What is man without the beasts? If all the beasts were gone, man would die from great loneliness of spirit. For whatever happens to the beasts, soon happens to man. All things are connected.

You must teach your children that the ground beneath their feet is the ashes of your grandfathers. So that they will respect the land, tell your children that the earth is rich with the lives of our kin. Teach your children what we have taught our children, that the earth is our mother. Whatsoever befalls the earth, befalls the sons of the earth. If men spit upon the ground, they spit upon themselves. I have seen a thousand buffaloes rotting on the prairie, left by the white man who shot them from a passing train. I am a savage and I do not understand how the smoking iron horse can be more important than the buffalo that we kill only to stay alive. This we know: The earth does not belong to man; man belongs to the earth. This we know. All things are connected like the blood which unites one family. All things are connected. Whatever befalls the earth befalls the sons of the earth. Man did not weave the web of life; he is merely a strand in it. Whatever he does to the web, he does to himself. Even the white man, whose God walks and talks with him as friend to friend, cannot be exempt from the common destiny. We may be brothers after all. We shall see.

One thing we know, which the white man may one day discover—our God is the same God. You may think now that you own Him as you wish to our land; but you cannot. He is the God of man, and His compassion is equal for the red man and the white. The earth is precious to Him, and to harm the earth is to heap contempt on its Creator. The whites too shall pass; perhaps sooner than all other tribes. Contaminate your bed, and you will one night suffocate in your own waste. But in your perishing you will shine brightly, fired by the strength of the God who brought you to this land and for some special purpose gave you domination over this land and over the red man.[7]

TALKING TO ANGELS?

Another way of moving into a closer relationship with God is to be in rapport with the spiritual beings that exist on the level of soul and assist humans and all life in evolution. I often ask in my lectures, "How many people believe in angels and that they are here to help us?" The hands are almost always unanimous or close to it (national surveys have indicated that 85% of the general population believe in angels). But when I ask, "How many communicate with them on a regular basis?" only a few hands are raised. If we believe in angels and that they are here to help us, why not be in communication with them on a very consistent basis? Most likely because of the old adage, "out of sight, out of mind." They may be out of sight but certainly not out of reach if we simply make an effort to be in contact with them.

The angelic, or devic kingdom as it is called in the East, is the spiritual dimension that is closest to us in the world of form and therefore is the most accessible. Be aware of the angelic life around you throughout your day. Open to the magic that exists in its energy. Talk to your angels and listen for their answers. You may hear words or receive impressions or perhaps the answers will come as symbolic experiences in your life. When we are in touch with the angelic kingdom, we can't help but be connected to our own soul.

We can also transcend this dimension to more subtle realms where guides and masters that have risen to higher levels of evolution can be contacted. I experience such contact as extremely subtle guidance in the form of thought impression or imagery that inspires me to higher understandings of my purpose and direction of my service in life. These higher beings of light are not as easily accessible as angels because their purpose is more broad and serves at levels more subtle and less involved with individual evolution than that of angels.

Gary Zukav, a renowned physicist and spiritual visionary, writes about inner guides or angels and "Teachers" in his excellent book *The Seat of the Soul.*

> Your soul knows its guides and Teachers. It drew upon their wisdom and compassion in charting the incarnation that became you, and that part of your soul that is you will be gathered into their waiting arms when the incarnation that is you comes to an end—when you go home. You receive loving guidance and assistance at each moment. At each moment you are prompted and encouraged to move into light.[8]

Below is a description of how I became aware of the spiritual beings that support my fulfillment in life and my soul purpose.

Several years ago, I was sparring in my kung fu class. I jumped and landed wrong, tearing the interior cruciate cartilage in my knee (according to later diagnosis). I rolled on the floor writhing in pain with my leg bent sideways at the knee in a 45° angle. As I continued to roll, it finally snapped back into place. I was filled with fear that I had damaged my knee to the point that I would not be able to continue the active lifestyle that I had enjoyed up until that point.

Normally, I would have applied some kind of spiritual healing technique to my leg as I was taken to the emergency room, but I was in too much pain to concentrate. I prayed. I cried out silently, "If there is any force out there that can hear me, please help me!" I heard a voice inside my head that simply said "Trust." So I did. I was surprised at hearing the voice and was convinced that it did not come from my own consciousness. I asked the voice, "Who are you?" "We are your angels" was the reply. I continued to communicate with them throughout my recovery.

When I was taken to the emergency room, the knee was so badly damaged that it again slipped out of place, bending sideways when they lifted it into position to be X-rayed. The look on the technician's face when this occurred was more horrifying than the pain in my leg, but I continued to trust. The first and second doctors whom I consulted both recommended major reconstructive surgery, and the MRI showed a clearly torn ligament. Both examinations showed movement of about three inches when my knee was pulled from side to side (not a good sign at all). My angels continued to say "Trust." I was on crutches for four weeks and purchased a brace to wear when I no longer needed them. I continued to pray and do healing work. A month later I consulted another doctor, and he thought I should try physical therapy and see how it goes. There was very little play in my knee by that time. So I began physical therapy and found that after a few months, as long as my hamstring was tight from doing regular exercise, the knee did not slip out of place. After about a year, my damaged right knee was stronger and more stable than my healthy left knee. I did not consult another doctor about my knee and have had no problem with it for over ten years.

From that point on, I began talking to my angels and asking them for guidance. I could give countless examples of miraculous occurrences that resulted from consulting them. One example is finding the exact home I wanted for exactly the price I wanted to pay after the 1992 Northridge earthquake. Housing was at a premium and almost impossible to find because of all of the displaced residents. I asked my angels, "Can you help me find a house?" "What kind of house do you want?" they asked." I responded, "I want it to be on a hill in the mountains." "How much do you want to pay?" they asked. "No more than I am paying now," I replied, which seemed impossible since I was sharing my rent with others who lived in a one-house community. Well, I got everything I asked for and lived in that house in the beautiful, rocky hills of Chatsworth for five years. Again, this is only one incident in hundreds.

What I have gleaned from more than ten years of communicating and receiving guidance and protection from these beings is that they exist around all of us. People from other cultures and beliefs call them by other names, but they are the same beings. To some few and gifted individuals, they may appear in physical form. Their appearance is most likely influenced by cultural conditioning and personal biases, but in truth, they are pure consciousness and are therefore formless.

Their sole (or soul) purpose and greatest joy is to assist us toward fulfillment and, even more so, toward service to others. Angels don't have to contemplate the truth that all life is connected. They live it. They do not know any other reality. When we communicate with angels, we are pulled into this reality—a reality beyond the physical plane and therefore not limited by physical laws.

I find that angels often answer questions with questions to help me become more clear about what I want. But they always answer if we choose to listen. Below is a message to you from the angels that have assisted me in my growth and service to others.

Message from Angels

We are here to assist you. Nothing offers us more delight than to help life forms to experience joy and growth. So many of you are close to us and ready to allow us to help you in creating fulfillment for yourselves and others, but you just don't realize we are here ready to offer our love and assistance. We do not have the ability to give you anything that you do not feel you deserve or that you are not ready for, but we can help you to grow in your recognition that you deserve all you desire that is right for you. We can assist you in receiving what you need most to grow and to share with others.

"What are you ready for that is eluding you or that you just haven't realized is possible? There is so much joy and fulfillment waiting for you. All you need to do is be open to it. Ask us for what you want; be open to the possibility. Affirm that you deserve it. Our greatest joy is to help you bring fulfillment to yourself and others. Just ask us. We will answer. We are all around you as you read this message. Feel our love. Feel our support. How can we support you right now in this moment? We love you completely.

Stop and talk to your angels after reading this paragraph. Be receptive to their answers. Don't analyze them. Ask why they are here. Whatever answer pops into your mind, trust it. If you don't understand the answer, ask for clarification, but don't try to analyze whether it is your answer or their answer; just be receptive and trust. What have you got to lose? Ask how they have supported you in the past. Ask how they can support you now and in the future. Ask for assistance in the important goals you have for your life. Ask them anything that will help you in your growth and expression of your soul.

5

The Magic
of Thought

Observe Your Thoughts

For free audio version, http://www.livingpurposeinstitute.com/meditation.htm

Close your eyes and observe your thought nature. Appreciate how incredible the power of your mind is, how you can process and store large amounts of information, how you can think abstractly, how quickly your mind can shift from one thought to another, how it never stops even when you want it to, and how you can organize thoughts into belief systems. Be aware of the untapped regions of your mind. What exists in these regions? Recognize that no matter how strong your beliefs may be, you can choose to change them. You can choose how you want to think and the quality of the thoughts you entertain. How could you use your mind in more magical ways? How often does your mind wander in fantasy? Run wild in obsessive worry? How would you like your mind to be? How often is your mind still, open to receiving inspiration from above? How often is it engaged in creative expression? Be thankful for the magical qualities of thought and affirm that you have the ability to direct your mind and choose your beliefs.

Affirm that you have thoughts, yet you are more than your thoughts.

How do you choose to use your thoughts?

✹   ✹   ✹

CREATING REALITY

As mentioned previously, the reality we experience is held in place by our thoughts and beliefs. The phrase "we create our own reality" is a common understanding in metaphysical thought. The self-fulfilling prophecy, as it is expressed in psychology, professes that whatever we expect of ourselves and life profoundly influences what we experience. Have you ever known someone who was a jinx? Everything just seems to go wrong for that person? We have all known people who seem lucky, where everything seems to go right for them. Are these extremes really just a matter of luck, or are they a result of attitude or belief?

I can't think of a better parable to illustrate the natural tendencies of the mind and the hold of our belief systems than Plato's cave, which was written as part of the brilliant Socratic Dialogues. Below is an abbreviated adaptation based on this classic:

A group of individuals was imprisoned in a cave from childhood. They were chained in a way that they could not move and could not see anything (including themselves and each other) except the cave wall in front of them. Behind them a fire burned continually, throwing a dim light upon the wall. Their only experience of the world was what they could hear and smell; sometimes they could see shadows projected on the wall in front of them. They believed that these experiences represented the world of reality.

Eventually, one of the captives was set free and was brought out of the cave into the sunlight. For some time, this individual was blinded by the light, unable to perceive the sunlit reality because of a lifetime lived in the darkness of the cave. In the beginning, he wanted to return to the darkness, where the harmless shadows would be a soothing comfort compared to the new, painful brilliance. In time, he was able to identify objects in the world of light and eventually even view and contemplate the sun's nature. He learned to cherish the new reality and see his past experience as a limited view of the world.

Then the individual ventured back into the cave to tell his former friends of the "real" world. It was now difficult for him to see in the darkness, and he could no longer relate to the understanding of his friends. He was mocked and called crazy for telling what were clearly lies or fantasies about the world beyond the cave.[1]

This is such a beautiful metaphor representing our perception of reality as a shadow of a richer world that is available to us all the time. Our first impressions of a freer world may be uncomfortable. We may find ourselves clinging to beliefs and patterns of the past because they are what we are used to—warm and cozy like old, comfortable clothes. As we see more and more of the real world, we recognize how limited our perception was previously. We often keep our experiences of this inner world to ourselves so that we are not ridiculed by those who have not seen it, and therefore may consider these experiences the rantings of a lunatic or, at best, a spiritual flake. We struggle at times with letting go of our past perceptions because we are so identified with them. But the more we taste the world of light, the more our interest in a shadowy past fades away and is replaced by a new world of brilliant beauty and joy.

Open to a world of brighter light.

While the spiritually wise have maintained for eons that our reality is conditioned by our beliefs, quantum theory has more recently come to the same conclusion. It has been determined through research that no observation of atomic energy can be analyzed without the assertion that the energy is changed by the mere process of it being observed. The scientist cannot be separated from the experiment. Our experience of the world is conditioned by our observation as well as our expectation. Fritjof Capra writes about the basic oneness of the universe and the role of the observer in *The Tao of Physics:*

> Quantum theory thus reveals a basic oneness of the universe. It shows that we cannot decompose the world into independently existing smallest units. As we penetrate into matter, nature does not show us any isolated "basic building blocks," but rather appears as a complicated web of relations between the various parts of the whole. These relations always include the observer in an essential way. The human observer constitutes the final link in the chain of observational processes, and the properties of any atomic object can only be understood in terms of the object's interaction with the observer.[2]

Deepak Chopra put it this way in an interview in *Meditation* magazine:

> There is no physical world. It's all a projection. The whole thing is quantum soup. Reality is pulling out from us rather than coming into us. It's pulling out just like light pours out from a bonfire or dreams pour out from a dreamer. In a dream state, you also project a certain world, but you say it's unreal. The waking world that you project out is also similarly projected by brain chemistry, which is a function of consciousness. So the fact is that the physical world is therefore never perceived quite the same by any two people.[3]

If the observer affects every observation and reality is pulling out from us, then our ability for affecting our experience of life is profound. In fact, what we experience is largely the result of what we expect. The universe feeds back to us our interpretation of it. This means that we are all masters of our reality. We all manifest our affirmations (conscious or unconscious) perfectly. If we want to be rich but we have an internal dialogue that breeds poverty, we will remain in poverty because we are unconsciously affirming that poverty is what we deserve. There are many cases of people who have won lotteries, who end up in poverty because they couldn't accept the wealth in their lives.

Whatever situation you find yourself in is likely a perfect reflection of your internal psyche. If you don't recognize your outer reality as a reflection of your inner dynamics, it is because they are occurring beneath the level of your awareness. Become more aware of your inner life and you will see the connection.

In The Carlos Castaneda series, Don Juan speaks often to Carlos about the power of our beliefs and our self-image or "personal history" over our limitations. In *Tales of Power*, he says to Carlos: "We live inside the bubble of our perceptions all of our lives and what we witness on its round walls is our own reflection."[4]

---

*Let your bubble of perception
dissolve and be free.*

Recognizing that we create our reality through our unconscious beliefs is an essential realization, because in it we can recognize our power. If we can create an undesirable reality through unconscious negative affirmation, we can just as easily create a desirable one through conscious choice. We can create affirmations and repeat them to replace those that we reinforce on an ongoing basis unconsciously. Sooner or later (let's affirm it is sooner), the new affirmations begin to become part of our unconscious content and then magic happens.

A Course in Miracles contains a workbook that offers a lesson for each day of the year.[5] It encourages us to live life each day embracing a specific, spiritual lesson and repeating an affirmation to reinforce it. I have found this to be a powerful force for change. We can also create our own daily curriculum for spiritual growth. We can intuit in meditation exactly what we need for our spiritual growth each day and commit to implement that growth. We can create and repeat affirmations throughout the day to help us achieve our intent.

Many metaphysical thinkers believe that *everything* that happens to us is a result of our belief system. I don't believe in such an extreme. We can greatly influence our experience by how we perceive the world, but there are some events that we cannot control because there are other influences on reality other than our own perceptions and beliefs. We can recognize that we can control much of our experience by taking responsibility for it, and for that over which we have no control, we can take responsibility for our *response*. We can choose to learn from every experience. In that choice comes acceptance, and recognizing the magic in the experience is the ultimate acceptance.

The Serenity Prayer, which is used frequently in twelve-step programs, offers a balanced insight into how to respond to that which we can control and that which we can accept.

> Lord, give me the serenity to accept the things I cannot change, the strength to change the things I can, and the wisdom to know the difference.[6]

As we evolve, we begin to see through the veil of form and the limitations of our fixed realities to the real world, just as the individual liberated from the cave was able to see more and more clearly in the world of light. One of the methods we can use to transcend the darkness of our limitations is affirmation.

THE POWER OF AFFIRMATION

The internal messages that condition our perception of the world are products of the reality we have accepted as a result of our past conditioning. The dialogue that goes on in the subtleties of our minds is the result of messages we heard repeatedly as children. These messages could have been communicated verbally or could have been communicated through feelings or body language. Whatever messages you hear most often in your head, you can be certain that they were conveyed to you in some way when you were young. We can counteract these internal negative affirmations by creating and repeating positive affirmations.

Create affirmations for anything you want to change about yourself or your life. Your affirmations are seeds that will grow into new behaviors and patterns. Moisten the soil with the water of your positive feelings that corresponds to the seeds of your affirmations.

Act from the confidence that comes
from the new feeling, and you will be new.

It may take time for the confidence to come that will inspire new ways of being, just as it takes time for a plant to take root and grow. Trust and be patient. Trusting that a goal will be accomplished, even if you don't know *how* it will be accomplished, is a powerful way to open to a world of soul magic.

Stop reading for a moment and consider what quality you need most in your life. Create a short phrase that affirms you already possess it. Make it an "I" statement. "I am loving." "I am abundant." The affirmation is the truth because you do possess the quality in your soul. The affirmation will be like a magnet drawing your soul power into your subconscious mind and ultimately, your reality. Now spanning the globe is a practice called The MAP: Manifesting Affirmation Process. You can access a free report on this supportive group process that creates Peace, Prosperity, and Perfect Health for you, your relations, and the world at www.affirmationmap.com

Every negative thought we have creates a negative reaction. Every negative judgment about someone or something creates a vibration of energy that decreases the power of the individual doing the judging. The negativity flows outward through the ethers having a restricting effect on all life because we are all connected. But we are all part of one grand system evolving step by step to a higher vibration of energy—a more positive force. Observe each negative thought you have and recognize it as a stepping stone to a higher understanding for yourself and for all evolving life. Recommit to choosing thoughts of acceptance, forgiveness, encouragement, and love. Forgive yourself in each moment and focus your intent toward higher expressions of love. You cannot be further along your path than you are. You are a perfect expression of evolving light in each moment of your ongoing evolution.

Every positive thought creates strength, healing, and light for the thinker and creates a nurturing effect on all life. Accept yourself the way you are and recognize that you can take a major step forward in this moment. You can choose a much more powerful use of your mind.

How would you like to use your mind?
Decide and make it so!
You have the power to choose.

You can also use your mind to affirm empowerment for others. When someone is talking to you about their problems, you can empower them (even if they are in denial or want to remain stuck in the problem) by refusing to buy into the problem. You can do this with empathy and, at the same time, affirm in your mind their ability to solve their problems. Sometimes it is more effective to do this without communicating it, because the communication may meet with resistance, but the affirmation can have a positive effect without their conscious knowledge. Just as we affirm a self-fulfilling prophecy for someone by agreeing with their negative self-image, we can release ourselves from that karmic struggle by letting go of our agreement with it and affirming a higher truth.

Below is an exercise that I have taught in many workshops. People have reported a tremendous effect when their higher truth is being affirmed in the midst of identifying with a problem. Try it with a partner in practice and then try it in real life whenever you have the opportunity.

※   ※   ※

Exercise for Affirming Another

Ask your partner to come up with a short phrase that affirms the integration of a quality they need in their lives. For example, if they need more love it could be, "I am filled with love." If they need more strength, it could be, "I am powerful." Then ask your partner to begin speaking about the biggest problem they are facing in their life. Listen to them with compassion, but do not buy into any limitations they may be expressing. Continue to inaudibly repeat their affirmation, recognizing their higher truth about the situation they are conveying. For example, if their affirmation is "I am at peace," you will continue to repeat internally, "You are at peace. You are at peace." Once your partner has completed their description of the problem, switch roles. After each of you has experienced the dynamic, talk about what you experienced in each role.

※   ※   ※

DIRECTING THE MIND

Joel Goldsmith, a metaphysical writer, outlines a plan for a seven-day, mental diet. The idea is to *try* to go for one whole week without a negative or destructive thought. Unless you are an enlightened master, it isn't likely that you will score a perfect 100. But the important feedback from the exercise is the awareness it creates about your thought process. Most people are amazed at how many negative thoughts they have in a day or even an hour. Through the intention of the exercise, the number of negative thoughts will reduce drastically by the end of the week. But why stop there? Notice how you feel at the end of the week with a more positive attitude. Affirm that you will always practice looking at life from a positive perspective.

Another great way to observe your mental processes is to stop each hour on the hour and observe the quality of your thoughts in different situations. A great technique for reminding yourself to do this is to set a timer or watch to ring every hour on the hour (or even every half hour). Watches can be purchased that have this specific feature. Each time the alarm goes off, notice the quality and the content of your thoughts. This will give you a clear picture of the kind of messages you give yourself in various situations.

Be aware of the thoughts that most often fill your head. What is your first thought when you are in conflict? How does your mind function when you are in a challenging situation? What fills your mind in the empty moments? What are the subtle thoughts going on beneath the surface when you are having a conversation? Notice in all of these situations, is the inner dialogue positive, uplifting, encouraging? Does it allow for wonder and awe? When is it negative or demeaning? When you make a mistake, does your internal dialogue say, "You idiot." Or does it say, "That's okay, come on, you can do better?"

As you continue this practice, you will most likely begin to anticipate the alarm and start adjusting your mental outlook before you even hear it. You can take this practice a step further. Upon the sounding of the alarm, or your anticipation of it, in addition to observing your mental process, consciously switch it to one of magical acceptance. Switch it to a state of awe and wonder. Be present in the moment and affirm that you are manifesting your highest potential.

Watch your mental process and train your silent dialogue to be nurturing to yourself and others. At first, your emotions may be in conflict with the new positive messages you are affirming because they have been conditioning you for many years, but eventually, the act of giving yourself unconscious positive messages will affect your entire being.

Through all of these techniques, we can recognize that we have a mind and we are more than our mind. We can practice training our mind to be receptive to the light of the soul. We can affirm over and over that the mind is an instrument of the soul and can be directed as a positive force in the world.

Once our mind becomes conditioned with a positive point of view, our ability to create magic becomes more acute. It becomes easier to see the magic in everything, and in fact, it can become a natural process. We can more easily direct our mind to create miracles in our life. Our visualizations and affirmations become second nature, even unconscious. Fulfilling goals and dreams becomes effortless when we approach them from a positive perspective. Our ability to influence others in positive ways also becomes more automatic.

The beauty of being human is that we have the opportunity through our mental focus to be connected with spiritual sources and at the same time be focused on the outer world. Practice infusing the world with spirit through your focused intent. Imagine that you are an equal-armed cross with an alignment that is both vertical, extending up into the heavens and down into the earth, as well as horizontal, extending outward across the plane of objective experience. Holding the tension between these two alignments is what creates spiritual presence in the world.

THE HIGHER MIND

The human mind has evolved considerably in its ability to analyze. Our society has aptly reinforced us in how to use our rational minds. Ninety-five percent of our formal education is geared toward rational imperative thought. Where and when do we learn how to think receptively, intuitively? In many cases, we are taught how not to: "Don't believe in fantasy. You have to be practical to make it in this world." I was held back in second grade because I "daydreamed too much." Thankfully, the corrective action did not impede my ability to dream. It did take me some time to recognize, however, that it was truly a talent, not a detriment. My natural ability to dream has greatly enhanced my creativity, my ability to write, to visualize, and to envision an ideal. We can help our children in their development by affirming their ability to dream, to create, to play. We don't have to buy into our culture's increasing tendencies toward struggle—working harder for less.

Challenge your cultural training. I once taught a seminar program called *Dare to Dream* (now called *Soul Purpose in Career*) in which I asked people to rediscover a dream that they had given up on. Many people have had dreams about what they want to do in life but let them go somewhere along the way out of "practicality"—out of a reinforced belief that they can't make a living doing what they truly love. We have dreams because we are here to live them! See chapter 10 for information and exercises to reclaim your dream.

Challenge and test your powers of intuition. The parts of our brain that are not used are the parts that our culture does not support us in using. How often are you struggling for an answer regarding a direction in your life and you actually ask the question, "What will happen in one year or five years if I choose this path?" How often are you searching for an answer to a philosophical question or a decision that may alter your future and you simply ask for an answer? Ask yourself the question right now. "What is the most important action I can take to assist me in my next phase of growth?" If you can't find your car keys, before getting frustrated and frantically searching for them (or afterward if you enjoy that kind of thing and you still haven't found them), simply try asking where they are. See if you get an answer, an impression.

As a director for more than seventy-five positions at a publishing company, I was constantly interviewing candidates for positions or promotions. Often there would be more than one qualified candidate for a position. In these cases, I would ask the hiring manager and/or supervisor to ask this question about each candidate (I would also ask myself the question), "What will be the outcome in two years from now if I choose this person for the job?" It was a way of intuiting each candidate's contribution into the future. Asking such a question would often lead to insights that would otherwise not be discovered. It might raise the intuition that an individual who has higher qualifications may be less likely to stay in the position or take the job as seriously as another candidate. The area of the business that was run by myself and the managers and supervisors that worked under me had the best hiring record in the company. Try this method for any important decision you need to make. Ask yourself what the outcome will be in three years, five years, for each option you have as a choice.

We have far more intuitive abilities than we might realize. When I was nineteen, I was doing some intense meditative training through which my intuitive abilities were greatly enhanced. During this time, while I was at work in a tennis shop, I had once had a thought that I recognized as self-demeaning. In that moment, I wondered where the thought was coming from because I wasn't in a negative frame of mind at all. I noticed that a co-worker was standing behind me, and I realized that it wasn't my thought I was registering; it was the co-worker's. It was a thought that I knew was consistent with his perception of me. From that point on, I became more aware of my ability to intuit the thoughts and feelings of those around me.

We may all read the thoughts and feelings of others more than we imagine, but we don't recognize it because we experience the thoughts and feelings as our own. This is easy to do, because our emotional and mental fields overlap and are not defined by the outline of our bodies. We can increase our intuitive abilities by practicing them. Just like any other skill, we can tone our subtle faculties by flexing our intuitive muscle.

While you are in the presence of someone, see if you can intuit what they are thinking or feeling. Just guess, and then ask them. See how close you are. If your ability is inaccurate at first, don't give up. If you gave up the first time you tried to read because you didn't do so well, you wouldn't be reading this book. There is a very persistent and relatively effective system in place for teaching us "practical" skills. By approaching our more subtle gifts with the same diligence as our analytical ones, we can profoundly affect our magical capability. We can only begin to imagine the capabilities of our minds if we use a larger part of our brains. Step out of the logical, sequential processes of the rational mind and discover a freer world with unlimited possibilities.

INTEGRATING WILL AND SURRENDER

There are times when it is necessary to focus our mind with the intent of our will like a laser beam for solving problems or tasks requiring concentration. The value of this capability should not be minimized. But when we are not concentrating, it is often more difficult to create that stillness that invites us into the world beneath the surface of analytical thinking—beneath the world of linear connections.

For some, there is a need to develop the will and the ability to focus the mind like a laser beam. Ultimately, we must learn to bal- ance our ability to surrender to a higher will and our ability to utilize our will, our power in the world. Imagine a state of being perfectly balanced in will and surrender. Another dichotomy, which when embraced, invokes our soul power. When we fuse surrender and will, we can open to the experience of effortless power. Imagine doing your daily tasks filled with personal power combined with the perfect peace of surrender to a higher power working through you. This state is truly a magical one. Take a moment to imagine being in this state on a regular basis. . . .

What is the proper balance of your will and surrender to a higher power? How can you fuse the two together? Think of examples of actions and reactions that combine both the serenity of surrender and the power of will.

The magician of the soul is one
who blends will and surrender perfectly.

The spiritual pacifist floats down the river, trusting that the river will guide the boat safely to its destination. There are often many surprises and disasters. The willful seeker fights against the current to force the boat precisely where it *should* go. This method is exhausting and may deplete life force prematurely. The magician of the soul surrenders to the flow of the river while skillfully using the oar of the will to guide the boat along the most efficient and magical pathway downstream.

If you need to develop your will and ability to focus your mind, there are many concentration exercises you can do. Practice multiplying a three-digit number by another three-digit number in your head on a regular basis. Practice seeing the etheric energy around people. Meditating on Symbols, the exercise in chapter 2, is the most powerful concentration exercise I have ever done. Another effective method is to choose a creative project and follow it through. The best practice is one that has practical value. Write a book. Learn a new skill.

If you need to still your mind and reach for higher levels of thought, give yourself the gift of serenity, of surrender. Let go of your need to control with your mind. How often have I learned through struggle that all I had to do was surrender to a higher power?

How much struggle does it take before you will surrender? What would happen if you surrendered at the beginning of struggle instead of at the climax?

Below is an exercise for creating balance between will and surrender. There is no wrong or right outcome from this exercise. When you have completed it, take some time to reflect on what the imagery means to you.

☀   ☀   ☀

Arrow Exercise

For free audio version, http://www.livingpurposeinstitute.com/meditation.htm

Close your eyes and imagine you have a bow and arrow. Twenty feet ahead of you is a target with rings and a bull's-eye in the center. Place the arrow against the string of the bow and, using all your might and will power, pull back the string, aim, and shoot the arrow. Notice where the

arrow lands. Now place another arrow in the bow. This time completely surrender to a higher power and, using no will of your own, pull back the string, aim, and shoot the arrow. Again notice where the arrow lands. Now place one final arrow in the bow, pull back the string, affirm a perfect balance between will and surrender, and let the arrow fly. Again notice where the arrow lands. What did you learn?

✸   ✸   ✸

In which case was your shot the most accurate? What does this say about the type of development that would be helpful to you at this point on your path? How can you use this metaphor to accomplish goals for which you are aiming, or to help you grow in any way?

THE STILL AND RECEPTIVE MIND

Imagine going though an entire day in a state of awe and wonder. Is it possible? What would it take? The term open-mindedness indicates such a magical state of being. We think of it in terms of being open to new or different ideas. I like to extend the definition of open-mindedness to include: a mind that is not only receptive to other ideas but to all that can be experienced in each moment. A mind that is open to the influence, the imagery, the whispering of the soul. A mind that is open to spiritual influences—guidance from angels and other spiritual beings. A mind that is open to the will of God—the Creative Principle blowing through the self like a calming breeze into the world of form.

I sometimes use the image of a funnel, imagining that my consciousness is reaching upward and outward into the heavens, open to the vast intelligence available in the universe. Try imagining your mind in this way. Feel your consciousness stretching, opening, receiving. Imagine that the funnel expands until it becomes inverted and your consciousness is now open and receptive 360° in all directions stretching even into the earth below you.

Stretch your awareness to its limit
. . . and then beyond,

To live in a mental state of awe and wonder, we must still the analytical mind. We must tame and educate its nature to control and to dwell in the past and project into the future. Not that these tendencies are negative, they simply need to be appropriated to their place of greatest efficiency. This aspect of growth has been the most challenging for me. My tendency has often been to project fear into the future—often about failing. As a result, I have found myself constantly searching for solutions to any and all perceived problems. This has had both positive and negative effects in my life. I have always been able to come up with creative solutions to challenges in the publishing business (of which there were many) as well as other areas of my life almost instantaneously. On the less healthy side, I have found myself unable to sleep while trying to solve problems. I often had some of my greatest solutions arrive at 3 o'clock in the morning, but almost no solution is worth sacrificing health and peace. I have experienced much stress as a result of this habit. But this challenge has been a great teacher by inspiring me to search for greater peace. It has been influential in developing the practice of the magic of the soul. My tendency toward mental busy-ness has been the motivation for me to search for greater peace of mind and, ultimately, to find the bliss that exists beneath the surface of analytical mental functioning.

A book that I consider the most important spiritual work I have read because of its profound and easy-to-apply philosophy is *The Power of Now* by Eckhart Tolle. In it, Tolle says this about the mind:

. . . the single most vital step on your journey toward enlightenment is this: learn to disidentify from your mind. Every time you create a gap in the stream of mind, the light of your consciousness grows stronger.

One day you may catch yourself smiling at the voice in your head, as you would smile at the antics of a child. This means that you no longer take the content of your mind all that seriously, as your sense of self does not depend on it.[7]

We can condition ourselves to a clearer, more effective use of our mind. The road to accomplish this is practicing stillness. Most everyone is proficient at using their mind to solve problems. But the larger area of growth is the least developed skill, which involves the quiet mind. Once we achieve a degree of a quiet and receptivity of mind, it is like a door is opened to the higher mind. When we can walk around with a clear mind, it is incredible how much more effectively it can be used. Intuition becomes easy as a space is created in the consciousness to receive more subtle mental impressions; there is less analytical activity using up the mental faculties. An image that has been helpful to me for the most efficient use of mental energy is capsulated in a poem I wrote many years ago.

The Fires of My Mind
The fires of my mind are not meant to be wisped about
by the winds of the will of others.
Nor are they to be consumed by the flames of social thinking.
Nor are they to be dowsed by the waters of untamed emotions.
They are to remain but a single flame held steady in the light of my soul.
Flickering only in harmony with divine purpose.

Once we succeed at stilling the mind through meditation or surrender, the peace we experience is beyond description. Today in my morning meditation, I reached a level of peace so profound I didn't want to leave it. I felt that the energy that I am beyond my self-identity was more real, more solid than how I experience myself in physical form. I was completely connected—no, more than connected—I was one in that moment with the energy of all life. Tears streamed down my face (as they are now while I write these words and re-experience the sensation) because the experience was filled with such beauty. But they were not "my" tears. They were the tears of all life flowing through a particular identification known as Patrick. I experienced my personality, or the personality of Patrick, as one aspect of that one life, no more or less important (and just as beautiful) in that moment than the grass it sat on, the trees surrounding it, or the wind flowing all around it.

You can use the two exercises below to guide the mind to a state of stillness and peace. Because they are presented sequentially on the audio CD, you can let the first exercise play directly into the second to enable a longer guided meditation, or pause the CD for some silent time before proceeding to the second version, or use them independently. As you practice these techniques, or other receptive meditation techniques listed in chapter 8, you can increase your ability to let your mind become a still flame held steady in the light of your soul. You can also use the first of these two as a prelude to other exercises on the CD. The relaxation technique at the beginning of this meditation is a good way to prepare body, emotions, and mind for any meditative technique.

❋   ❋   ❋

Exercise for Stilling the Mind
(Track 6 on Audio CD)

Take ten deep breaths. Fill your lungs completely. Exhale until there is no air left. Watch your breath. . . . With each breath, feel yourself become more relaxed, cleansed, purified. Take a deep breath and hold it. Tighten your jaw muscles. Raise your eyes to the top of your head. Release your breath. Relax your eyes and facial muscles. Be aware of a tingling sensation at the top of your head. Imagine a golden yellow light is causing the tingling sensation. Feel it move downward through your scalp and forehead.

Everywhere it goes, it brings a relaxing and healing sensation. Feel it soothing the tiny muscles in and around your eyes. Behind your eyes. Deep into the cells of your brain. Feel it spreading through your facial muscles. Your jaws. The top of your neck in front and back. Feel it flowing through all the tiny muscles in your neck and down through your shoulders as they go limp. It continues down through your upper arms, your elbows, your forearms, wrists, hands, and fingers. The tingling sensation continues through your chest and upper back—deep into your muscle tissue. The light tingles as it cleanses your bronchial tubes, lungs, and your heart. It flows downward through your solar plexus, cleansing your pancreas, liver, spleen, the muscles in your stomach and back. The tingling light massages your kidneys and moves downward through your buttocks, your abdomen, your intestines, your genitals. The flow streams into your upper legs, deep into the muscles, through the knee joints, your calves, ankles, feet, and toes. You have now reached complete physical relaxation.

Feel your awareness become lighter than the element of the earth of your body.

A wave of calmness flows through your emotional nature. All of your feelings become more and more calm until you reach a point of complete emotional tranquility— just like a completely motionless woodland pool of water with a surface as smooth as glass.

Feel your awareness become lighter than the water of your emotions.

A breeze of peace flows through your mental nature. Your mental processes begin to move slower . . . and slower . . . and slower—more and more clear and receptive until you reach a point of complete mental stillness. Like a still candle flame held steady in the light of your soul.

Feel your awareness become lighter than the fire of your mind.

Feel your awareness become as light as the air of your spirit.

Lighter than earth. Lighter than water. Lighter than fire. Your awareness is as light and expansive as air. It continues to become lighter, thinner. . . . Your awareness is now lighter than air.

No body. No feeling. No thought. No being.

Nothing.

❉   ❉   ❉

Exercise II for Stilling the Mind
(Track 7 on Audio CD)

Your physical, emotional, and mental bodies are still at peace and in harmony with the vibration of your soul. Imagine that you are standing on a mountaintop at night. Your body becomes lighter and lighter, and you realize that you are no longer physical, but a bubble of thin moisture. You lift off of the earth into the night sky. As you rise higher and higher, your awareness contained in the bubble becomes lighter and lighter and the walls of the bubble, thinner and thinner. Your awareness includes more and more space as the bubble expands further and further. Finally, the bubble containing your awareness ever so gently dissolves with a silent pop, and your awareness is released to stretch through the infinite universe. Allow your awareness to be . . . limitless . . . unbound by mental constraints . . . just being . . . one with all.

❉   ❉   ❉

6

The Magic of Feeling

❋ ❋ ❋

Observe Your Emotions

Observe your feeling nature. Be aware of the different feelings you have experienced in this day. Notice how intense your emotions can be at times. Notice how powerful your love can be. Let the love in your heart well up and overflow out of you in all directions. . . . Remember times when your feelings overwhelmed you. Think of times when you were able to direct your emotions skillfully. Recognize that you can choose how you wish to feel. Appreciate the magic in your feeling.

Affirm that you have feelings, yet you are more than your feelings.

How do you choose to live your feelings?

❋ ❋ ❋

THE POWER OF LOVE

Perhaps the greatest lesson I learned from Dr. Barnum, a teacher whom I studied with from 1980 until his death in 1985, is a message that I haven't heard expressed quite the way he did. He taught that our natural state is one of unconditional love, and in all the time I knew him, he walked his talk in how he lived his life. He said, "When we are in our natural state, we express love in everything we do and to everyone we are in contact with. If we are not experiencing love flowing through us, then we are blocking it either consciously or unconsciously. It actually takes an effort, a tension on our part, to stop that flow of love." This truth has powerful ramifications. It means that in order to experience the bliss of love flowing through us, all we must do is let go. All we have to do is give in to it! Sounds so simple, doesn't it?

Give in to your love in this moment.
Let go of whatever stands in its way.

It has been written and proclaimed over and over that there is no greater power than love. It is one of the themes depicted in almost all novels and movies. How amazing to have such a power available to us, so close to us that all we have to do is open our hearts. And once we do, we recognize how much easier life is. I'm sure you have experienced at some time or another what it is like to be holding a grudge or feeling anger about someone or something and you finally decide to just let it go. What a relief it is. The entire body relaxes. Have you ever taken it a step further and decided to replace the grudge with love? Jesus Christ said, "Love your enemies." What a powerful statement! What a powerful practice! If you succeed, you may find that your enemies are no longer enemies. Some may become your closest friends. Some unhealthy relationships may just drop away as you let go of the friction that keeps you karmically tied to certain individuals.

About whom in your life are you holding energy that you could forgive and free your heart? Forgiveness isn't as much about the other person as it is about you. Let go of the anger (expressing it first if you need to) and allow your love to flow to that person, either directly through communication or simply through your intention.

Let your heart be free.

I recently visited the Los Angeles Buddhist Vihara in Pasadena with a friend who is a member of the temple. I spoke with Venerable Ahangama Sri Dhammarama. He is the leader of his order in the United States and Canada and is a respected Buddhist teacher. I asked him how he remained at peace through the challenges of life. His answer was so simple and encapsulates all we really need to do to open to the magic of the soul: "practice loving kindness." If we practice loving kindness in everything we do, our lives will be filled with the power of spirit, because we are in perfect harmony with the way in which God energy expresses itself in the world.

We can practice loving kindness even in times of conflict. A dear friend of mine used to work in a beauty salon as a hair stylist. She had a customer who was generally perceived as an extremely bitter and obnoxious old woman. Everyone in the salon dreaded when she walked through the door, because she would always complain about something or someone who had treated her unfairly. Once you create a label, it is very difficult to get rid of it, because people expect you to behave a certain way.

This friend of mine is the most forgiving and kind person I have ever known, so she had a difficult time dealing with the abrasive woman. She would try her best to direct her customer's negative comments into something positive but with little success.

She was taking a class in *A Course in Miracles* and decided to apply one of the lessons to her situation at work. In her daily meditations, she imagined sending love and acceptance to the difficult customer. The next time the elderly woman came in, she appeared to be an incredibly friendly and delightful person. Even my friend's co-workers, who had no idea of the exercise, commented later about the miraculous change. It was without question the first time she had ever seen this woman really happy. Was this a coincidence? Did the woman change completely or just in the presence of my friend, the one who sent the love? Perhaps the answer is both. My friend's experience of the woman changed as she released her expectation and tension arbout the woman. And perhaps it did change the woman at least to some degree. We can never overestimate the power of love.

Being loving to people, however, doesn't mean we should allow people to walk all over us. In addition to compassionate love, we can also apply strong love and wise love. It is not loving to enable people to be weak by allowing them to treat us unfairly as a result of their unhealthy behavior. We are not committing a loving act if we do not speak out against injustice when we see it. But even in the midst of creating healthy boundaries and standing up for what is right, we can do so with love.

Is it possible to love and fight at the same time? Most martial arts training, if it is still connected with its origin, is a practice of peace. Battle is only considered a last resort and a matter of self-defense. In aikido, the goal is not only to keep the self from harm but also to keep the attacker from harm. Setting boundaries is an act of self-love. Setting them skillfully is an act of compassionate love.

RELEASING TRAPPED EMOTION

While it is true that we can surrender at any moment to a higher power, to the love that is our nature, it is often helpful or even necessary to explore and release the blocks that crop up as a barrier. In fact, the more we set our intention to be a light in the world, the more clearly will be illuminated the darkness within us that we must heal in order to brighten our radiance. The act of exploring and releasing emotional blocks is an act that combines our will and ability to surrender—a conscious surrendering.

Imagine a log jam representing a block in the river of your flowing love. Each time you surrender, more water flows over the top of the dam. But once you remove the dam, it takes less effort to surrender. The water flows evenly without a conscious effort to let go.

It is difficult to perform magic while unconsciously holding onto emotional blocks. We may visualize success and even believe in our mind that it is possible, even probable, but darkness that exists in our lower unconscious (repressed feelings that we all have to some degree) creates a barrier that keeps our magic from fully blossoming. These blocks are actually part of the magical process and often hold the very keys to their release.

Through years of counseling and helping people to access and heal the content of their lower unconscious or shadow self, I have noticed a significant dynamic. The transpersonal qualities that the individual needs to develop in their growth are usually trapped along with the corresponding "negative" emotion that is repressed in the lower unconscious. I have observed that as individuals embrace and release their pain, they automatically open to a higher expression of compassion. As they tap into their anger or rage, they become more powerful in their lives. As they address their fears, they become more creative and self-actualized. I have found this in my own emotional healing as well.

If a person has deep pain, for example, that they have repressed from childhood, they often have a block to being compassionate with themselves and others. One reason that any feeling might be repressed is a belief or attitude (often unconscious) that it is not okay to have that feeling. Therefore, it is usually not okay for others to have that feeling either. When an individual embraces and releases their pain, they will naturally feel compassion for themselves. The mere act of releasing is a statement that it is okay to have the feeling. The powerful and freeing experience that accompanies the release reaffirms that it is not only okay but extremely healthy to have and express the emotion. In addition, they will naturally increase their compassion for others as they experience how beneficial it is to be compassionate to themselves. In simpler terms, the heart opens.

*Release and open and
let unlimited compassion flow through you.*

Freeing the transpersonal quality that has been locked away with a repressed emotion can be even more dynamic in relation to anger. People who have a lot of repressed anger often have a hard time confronting people or creating healthy boundaries. In an extreme example, these people will do anything to avoid conflict because they were taught that anger should not be expressed. When their anger or even rage is embraced and released through cathartic process, they can be shocked by the amount of energy they gain in their lives. There is power in anger, and the power gets locked away with the anger when it is repressed. Suddenly, they are more willing to be confrontational (sometimes awkwardly at first, as it is a new skill) in appropriate situations in their life. The energy and freedom in the release affirms that expressing anger can be a healthy and necessary function of being human when directed responsibly.

Let your emotion out.
It deserves to be free.
You deserve to be free.

Releasing repressed emotions has been an important part of my spiritual path. As a teenager and young adult, I repressed my feelings of pain, inadequacy, and anger. It took many years of releasing trapped emotions to arrive at a place of greater emotional freedom. I learned to honor all the feelings I had repressed. I learned that they contained powerful positive forces that had been locked away in my unconscious. When I first recognized in my early twenties that I was repressing a lot of fear, I decided to tell everyone with whom I came in contact that I was experiencing fear. It took great courage to do so, and I learned to recognize that strength did not come from the absence of fear but through the acceptance of my fear. I also recognized that my propensity to repress emotions is a gift that has led me to search for greater freedom and has inspired me to help others access their inner feelings.

When I began embracing and releasing repressed emotions from childhood (maybe even from past lives), it was a freeing experience. It was as if a giant weight filled with tension was released from my being. Each emotion of pain, fear, or anger that came up from my lower unconscious turned out to be far less frightening than I had imagined, considering the energy it took to hold them in place. I began to appreciate my humanness and embrace all of my weaknesses. I became a more grounded individual. I learned that at the core of my being, what exists is not only light but also darkness. My shadow, which contains all of my weaknesses, is an important part of who I am, and by embracing it, I become more whole. By letting out the darkness, it becomes exposed to the light. This is an ongoing process, and periodically, I am confronted with my own shadow and my own resistance to it. Each time I am willing to see my weak- nesses honestly, I become freer. Each time I accept my deepest inner antithesis of soul, I become more whole.

We all have a dark side or shadow self that contains our hatreds, prejudices, judgments, resistances, cruelties, jealousies, fears, and angers or rage. We come face to face with our shadow at different points in our lives through feedback from others, deep self-reflection, or messages from our dreams. Because of the propensity of the ego to present the self-image in the most favorable light, we may often discount or deny the shadow in these instances. If we open to our shadow self, however, we come to know ourselves at a truly deep level.

Carl Jung went so far as to suggest that our entrance into the social unconscious, our connection to everyone and everything, can be through the "narrow door" of the shadow as illustrated in this passage.

> The meeting with oneself is, at first, the meeting with one's own shadow. The shadow is a tight passage, a narrow door, whose painful constriction no one is spared who goes down to the deep well. But one must learn to know oneself in order to know who one is. For what comes after the door is, surprisingly enough, a boundless expanse full of unprecedented uncertainty, with apparently no inside and no outside, no above and no below, no here and no there,

no mine and no thine, no good and no bad. It is the world of water, where all life floats in suspension; where the realm of the sympathetic system, the soul of everything living, begins; where I am indivisibly this and that; where I experience the other in myself and the other-than-myself experiences me.[1]

By accessing the shadow parts of ourselves, we free them to be healed and integrated. One definition of evil is the repression of darkness. The most dangerous individuals are those who are in steadfast denial of their darkness. By not recognizing their potential for evil, they end up expressing it disguised as good. Hitler convinced many that his mission was one of benevolence. He would make the world a better place through ethnic cleansing. History is filled with accounts of individuals who performed evil acts in the name of justice, morality, or even God.

When we open to our shadow, we accept ourselves. Self-esteem is simply the act of loving ourselves, and truly loving ourselves means that we love even the most unlovable parts of ourselves. We connect to others and everything through the recognition of our light but also through the recognition of our darkness. If we are in denial of our darkness and see ourselves only as light, we will separate ourselves emotionally from everyone in whom we see darkness or weakness. When we recognize our own darkness, we connect with the darkness in others and we are empowered to heal both. Recognizing our light is the magic of the soul. Embracing our darkness is the magic of being human. Both are important on this journey we call life.

Embrace your emotions and shadow as much as you need to and for as long as you need to but don't go to an extreme. Because the release is freeing, some people get addicted to the release without moving to a higher level of healing. Each time you release emotion, be open to the idea that you are free. Do further release only if and when you recognize a need. The need for release may go in cycles. Be aware of your inner world and give yourself the support and nurturing you need when you need it.

We can begin to embrace our shadow simply by becoming aware of the emotions that we have suppressed. The exercise below is an extremely powerful one that I developed and found invaluable as a tool for emotional catharsis.

❋   ❋   ❋

Exercise for Emotional Release

Go to a place where you can be completely alone—a deserted park, an isolated beach, a field in the mountains—someplace where you can run wildly and scream without concern for what people will think. Run as fast as you can for as long as you can (even if it is not very fast or very far) and notice how the running feels to your body. Walk until you catch your breath. As you walk, just feel your body. Repeat this several times until your body is ready for rest. Lie down and spread your arms and legs. Open yourself to the sun's light (even if it is not sunny). Breathe deeply and become aware of any tension. Press the spot where the tension exists and increase the sensation of the tension. Allow the sound that represents the tension to come out of your body, whether it be moaning, crying, screaming, laughing, grunting, and so on. Intensify the feelings associated with the tension as you release the sound. Encourage yourself to let out all the emotion that is stored in your cellular memory. Allow images associated with the feelings to come into your awareness. They may be images from recent emotional crises, childhood traumas, past life experiences (if you believe in them), or symbolic events (that may not have any conscious memory attached to them but are real in your mind). Continue to allow and encourage the release of the emotions and associated sounds. Let the emotional release change (angry screams to painful sobs to fearful whimpers, etc.). Give your emotions complete freedom to express.

Once you feel peace in an area of tension, explore other areas in your body. Common places of tension are the abdomen, stomach, solar plexus, heart, thymus, throat, and head (especially the temples). Press each area and release the tension and emotional energy.

When you have let go as much as you can, again open to the sun's warm light. Allow yourself to be filled with healing energy. Be open to the qualities that you want to replace the energy that you have released (this is very important because if you don't replace that which is released, it will fill itself with what it is most familiar). Pull in from the heavens above you and the earth below you the energies of light, life, strength, compassion, love, creativity, and self-reliance—all the qualities that you need most in your life. Imagine yourself surrounded by nurturing, loving guides or angels that heal you gently with their encouraging words and touch.

I conducted the above exercise in the mountains during a seminar called *Primal Fire Intensive*. Many people who were ready to release their trapped emotion had amazing peak experiences and felt more in touch with their bodies and souls than they ever had in their lives. For those wishing to explore and release emotions of the past, I recommend doing this exercise at least once a week for a month or two when you begin (I performed it several times a week during my most intense period of emotional clearing). Combining the release with exercise is the ideal way to conduct this process, but you may modify it to fit your needs. You can perform it in your home and combine it with other forms of exercise. The emotional release can be achieved without physical exercise, but the physical exertion puts the body in an energized yet peaceful state. The exertion can also reduce both physical and emotional resistance and prime the psyche for allowing new possibilities.

Clearing emotion can also be as simple as becoming aware of an emotional tension and releasing it when you are in a safe place. With practice, it becomes easy to access the emotion needing release. You can even try it while driving. Be sure to continue to drive safely, of course. It is an effective environment because no one can hear your screams or notice if you are crying. In our busy days, there is little time to be in touch with our physical and emotional tensions. Take time to be in touch with them and give them the release and nurturing they need and deserve.

HONORING AND ACCEPTING FEELINGS

So how does all this releasing of emotion fit into a spiritual practice? Aha! Another dichotomy. How do we strive for peace and still embrace and release anger, for example? We can honor all our feelings as important aspects of our evolving self even though we want to grow toward increasingly positive expressions of emotion.

Understanding and directing the feeling nature is one of the most challenging aspects of being human. In terms of interpersonal relationships, it is not the challenges between individuals that are as relevant to the health of a given relationship as much as it is the way in which we exchange our emotions regarding those challenges.

Many systems teach that we should rise above our negative emotions or transmute them to higher feelings—transmute anger to forgiveness or love, fear to courage, and pain to trust or surrender. I agree with this philosophy, *if* we are able to do so without suppressing. There is a subtle distinction between transmutation and suppression (conscious) or repression (unconscious). In the long run, it is healthier to release emotion in the moment than it is to build it up and then have to do some crazy running and screaming exercise to release it later. Of course, we cannot live in our society releasing all of our emotions all the time and also be practical. For example, we don't want to express our anger passionately at our bosses or cry in front them (unless they happen to be a really cool boss). As a corporate manager, I encouraged such behavior and always had tissues handy at one-on-one meetings. This is a rare exception in the corporate world, however. But we can always express our emotion at a level of diplomacy that fits the situation.

If we choose to transmute our anger to forgiveness and see the magic in the situation but we are so filled with rage that we are shaking as we "recognize the fricking magic in the situation," then we are really just repressing. Whatever emotional response brings the greatest feeling of peace and freedom is generally the healthiest choice for where we are in any particular moment. Each situation in which we find ourselves that brings up strong emotion may require a different response depending on where we are and the strength of the emotional trigger. But the more consciously we make each choice to respond, the more we will learn and find ourselves more readily choosing more magical and empowering responses with greater and greater ease.

If we can express the fullness of our emotions in a healthy way as soon as we feel them (or as soon as possible if it is not appropriate in the moment), we will free ourselves from further repression. We also open a direct flow from our soul, because by expressing who we are in the moment, we are accepting ourselves—honoring ourselves—allowing our Self to flow into the world. We free energy that is tied up in the tension between holding the emotion and its silent cry for release. When we free the energy, we have more power.

Gary Zukav speaks about the spiritual value of emotional cleansing in *The Seat of the Soul.*

> By keeping your emotions clear, emotional negativity does not reside in you, and you become lighter and lighter. This opens your intuitive track because it allows you a clear sense of loving. It brings you closer to unconditional love and renders you harmless. It lightens the quality of your frequency, so to speak, and therefore the guidance that you receive is clear and unobstructed as it enters your system.[2]

All of our emotions exist for good reason. For example: We have anger to focus our power toward resolution. We have pain to help us grow by teaching us to make choices that lead to healthier living. We have fear to guide us away from danger. So, it is essential that we honor our emotions as our teachers, and also guide them with the wisdom we gain from their lessons. Let me repeat that because it is an important point: It is essential that we honor our feelings as our teachers and also guide them with the wisdom we gain from their lessons. With each lesson we embrace consciously, we can rise to higher levels of ability to transmute our feelings to a higher frequency.

The most effective way to deal with emotions is to *feel* them fully. There is a wide range of responses that can be inspired by various feelings, but regardless of the response we choose (consciously or unconsciously), our freedom and wisdom will be greater if we allow ourselves to feel the depth of our emotions and learn from what they tell us. The important thing to remember is that none of them are wrong and that they can all be honored and appreciated.

Relax and trust that every experience brings you to a higher expression of light.

Transmutation, or an ability to raise the emotion to a higher vibration, is possible. We can rise to a level of acceptance that will transcend the need to process emotion in usual ways through embracing and applying a higher principle, such as forgiveness over anger. An example of accepting an event that would create an angry (if not bitter) reaction in most people is inherent in this account of an accident, the healing, and ultimately the death of my dear friend and psychosynthesis teacher, Dr. Vivian King. This woman was a teacher of teachers who empowered hundreds of therapists and others in the healing professions through the techniques of transpersonal therapy. She had a profound ability to access her soul and express it in her work and her life.

Vivian was hit by a drunk driver and suffered extensive head and brainstem trauma about two and a half years ago. She was in a coma for three months. When she first came to, her head was as large as a basketball from swelling. When she was transported to California six months after the accident, I visited her in the hospital. She had no movement in her hands and legs and also had lost the ability to speak. Her head and face were still quite contorted from the trauma. Her mental functions, however, were perfect, which is rare for coma victims who are unconscious as long as she was. She could communicate with the help of a laser pen that was strapped to a pair of reading glasses. She used the pen to point (by moving her head) to letters on a chart fashioned after a keyboard.

That day, she and her caseworkers were deciding where she would relocate as she would be moving to a full-care facility. Synchronistically (and by no accident, I would pose), she was moved to a facility only five minutes from my house. I was able to visit her frequently to do healing work and to learn even more from this woman who I believe was a living saint.

She underwent physical therapy, and her facial features improved. Over the next year, she became able to move her legs only fractionally and her fingers well enough to type on a keyboard. She was also trained to speak in whispers using her breath, as she never regained the use of her vocal chords. With the help of an amplifier and a trained ear, one could learn to understand her but not without extreme concentration.

I spent many hours a week with her, and during one of our early meetings, I asked her if she was angry at the drunk driver who had crippled her. She looked at me kind of puzzled and replied, "No, I have too many more important things to think about." She added quite peacefully, "I do wish he had adequate insurance to cover my medical bills, though."

Through the tragedy, Vivian lost her love relationship, the use of her body, her possessions, her ability to serve in the way she had before, and ultimately, her life. She said at one point that she had become a teacher who could not speak and a writer who could not write. She was treated by most of her health care professionals as "a child." She was often treated as someone who could no longer think for herself, which can happen frequently to people who have disabilities, especially those who have a limited ability to communicate. Yet through all of it, she never blamed anyone. She did become angry at times over the way people treated her, but she would always reach a place of peace, and she consistently looked for ways that she could grow from the lessons of her limitations.

She inspired her friends and her nurses with her continuous compassion for others and her ability to still laugh through her challenges. I would marvel at how she would perform the almost impossible task of feeding herself with a retractable mechanical arm, having food all over her face and falling onto her bib, all the while smiling or even laughing at the absurdity of it all.

She showed little improvement after the first year of rehabilitation and accepted that she would never in this lifetime recover her physical capabilities. She decided to continue to live for a while to remain "a force of peace" in the world. Eventually, though, she decided that her body had become like a prison, and she longed to dance again. She decided to leave her body by ceasing to take food or liquid.

Although I had wished she had chosen differently, I supported her decision. I signed the legal document declaring that she would refuse medical treatment. I experienced her decision as a clear choice of moving toward a greater life rather than one of running away from her present life. In the visits I had with her shortly before her death, she seemed at a place of complete peace. It was quite inspirational being in the presence of someone who had absolutely no attachment to life. She systematically sold or gave away all her possessions. She purposely prepared to leave everything she had accumulated and built, physically and emotionally, in her life. Her leaving was much harder than she had expected it to be, as were the last years of her life. Now she dances again with angels' wings to lift her high above the ballroom of physical life.

Any example of moving from anger to acceptance is a testimony to the magic of the soul. For someone to have lost as much as Vivian and, at the same time, accept while continuing to empower herself and others attests to the unlimited power of the human spirit.

FEAR AND PAIN

Fear is perhaps the most debilitating of emotions. The phrase "paralyzed by fear" illustrates how powerful it can be. After disasters like earthquakes or hurricanes, people can be almost literally paralyzed and afraid to leave their homes.

Fear can also be a powerful force on a subtle level. As a child, I didn't feel accepted by my father. I was never able to work this dynamic out with him in life because he died when I was seven. I spent much of my life resisting and, at the same time, trying to prove my worthiness, often in ways that were not healthy for me. I would look for approval from others. I would get extremely stressed at times out of the fear (often unconscious) of failing at anything. Even though I recognized the fear many times and did much inner work to release it, it persisted for years and still affects me in subtle ways. I don't think we ever completely outgrow our emotional challenges in life. It is not a process of getting to some end result, but a process of unfolding, like the petals of a flower opening to more and more light.

A pivotal moment in healing the emotional rift between my father and me happened a few years ago when I was on a spiritual journey that landed me at Findhorn, a world-famous spiritual community in Northern Scotland. I was going through some major soul searching and transformation. It was at the height of my illness. I was extremely sick and I didn't know why, and nothing I had done up to that point had helped. I identified with my father because he was sick for three years before being diagnosed with liver cancer, and he died relatively soon after the diagnosis. Because of my own experience, I could better understand his confusion about his illness and the pain of knowing he would lose his life and all those he loved. I also remembered my own pain at not being able to see him before he died. He didn't want my sister or me to see him dying but to remember him in a healthier state.

I did some emotional release around this issue and imagined myself visiting him in his hospital bed (which never actually happened). I held his hand and told him I loved him as he died. This symbolic interaction was one of the most tender and meaningful moments in my life. Below is the letter I wrote to him directly after this self-guided process.

Dear Dad, I now appreciate the pain and anguish you must have gone through when you were sick with cancer. You were always so strong and healthy before. How frustrating to have no idea of what was wrong and not be able to heal. It must have seemed like you were crazy. And then to find out it was cancer and to know you were going to die leaving behind a wife and two children. How incredibly sad and tragic. All this time, I only thought of what I didn't get from you. I never thought of your pain. I wish I could have comforted you somehow. I miss you Dad. I wish I could have known you better. I guess I did not grieve your death because I feared that had you lived, I would not have been accepted by you, and at some level thought I had escaped your judgement. But of course I carried that perceived judgement around with me all my life anyway. If you had been alive, maybe we could have worked it out somehow. I love you Dad, and I am sorry I withheld my love all these years. I know you did the best you could, and I know you have grown from your experience here. I hope we meet again and can complete what we started together. If you can from where you are, please help me to be strong. Teach me what it is like to be a man. I was never really taught and it has been so hard to learn on my own. You have probably been helping me all along, but I have never accepted your help until now. I want to be well again and healthy and strong like you once were. I feel your presence here with me Dad. Thank you for being my father. I love you.

I cried throughout the writing of this letter. In his reply, I intuited the message that he was proud of me, that he admired what I had done with my life, and that he had learned from *me* what it was to be a good man. From that moment on, I felt his presence more closely than I ever had since his death. I felt him guiding me and supporting me, which I believe he had done in some way all my life, but I had never before opened to it.

We can heal our fears from the past through imagery and release. In other cases, a cathartic process may not even be necessary. We can recognize that there is healthy fear, which causes us to be cautious of immediate impending danger or to react with heightened awareness when threatened. But there is also unhealthy fear, which is based on events of the past that are no longer threatening or projections of what might happen in the future. In many cases of these unrealistic fears, we can honor them as indicators of past conditioning and let them go. We can simply recognize that fear is an acronym for

False
Evidence
Appearing
Real

We can use each and every realization of fear as a reminder to be present in the here and now. We can experience the magic in the moment rather than be controlled by a fear based on the past or future. We can be compassionate toward our fear and recognize that it too is part of our ongoing process of growth. Each realization of fear, each expression, and each release leads us further along our path of realization of the magic in life.

Whenever possible, express your fear when you experience it. You will find it often dissolves in the process of identifying it. Certainly the fear of fear can be more ferocious than fear itself. When we let go of our resistance by being willing to embrace and express it, we affirm that we are stronger than it is. It cannot hurt us. By acknowledging and honoring our fear, we are pulled into the present moment and opened to the magic that can be experienced in our process of liberation.

Ekhart Tolle says this about fear in *The Power of Now*:

> Is fear preventing you from taking action? Acknowledge the fear, watch it, take your attention into it, be fully present with it.

Doing so cuts the link between the fear and your thinking. Don't let the fear rise up into your mind. Use the power of the now. Fear cannot prevail against it.[3]

Recently I noticed that as a result of practicing the magic of the soul that I rarely feel fear anymore whether on a subtle or obvious level. Because I look for the magic or growth in every moment, I no longer project into the future fears about what might happen. Through recognizing the blessing in my most challenging moments, I know that I will gain growth from whatever challenges life may hand me in the future. This is not to say that I never feel fear, but it has gone from a consistent subtle motivation (and sometimes over-whelming dread) to a nonfactor. As a result, I am in a consistent state of freedom.

When we do have pain, we practice expressing it in the moment. Whenever possible and whenever it is safe (or sometimes even if you're not sure but want to take a risk), express your pain. I was told a story about a female executive who was criticized unfairly in a corporate meeting. She began to weep and some came to her rescue with comfort. She said, "Please leave me. I don't need help right now. This is how I express my anger and pain." Her peers (mostly men) were struck and some were inspired by this woman's power. She was not at all ashamed by her choice to resolve her emotions openly. I also know of cases when such a display of emotion in the workplace has had the opposite effect. So use wisdom in determining what a safe environment is. We all have been inspired by others when they express their vulnerability. I have seen men cry in the middle of a public speech that brought the entire audience into rapport with the speaker. Honor yourself by honoring your pain.

Honor your pain and recognize
that you have the power to heal it.

Rather than replacing anger, hurt, or fear with spiritual energy—light—try acknowledging and accepting the emotion and allowing your darkness and light to come together. The light will heal the darkness, and the darkness will ground and enrich the light just like when the sun and the earth are united by the birth of a flower that stretches its roots into the dark soil and its petals toward the sun's light.

COMMUNICATION

We can learn to direct our emotions without suppressing them. The process that leads to such an ideal requires finding a balance between allowing the emotions to be, without being controlled by them. The key to balance is conscious choice. When we react rather than respond, we are identified with our emotions. If we disidentify from them, we have the ability to direct them through choice. By disidentify, I do not mean a detachment that removes us from emotion but simply a stepping back and then moving into whatever emotion we choose with as much passion as we choose.

Once, I was involved in a conversation with a printer in the office of *Meditation* magazine. I felt the printer should take responsibility for an error they made by reducing the cost of the job. He argued his side of the point, and it seemed as though he wasn't really listening to me. So I raised my voice in anger, which got his attention. There was a moment of tension (that I was purposely creating) between us that led to a resolution partially out of a mutual desire to release the tension.

Directly after the incident, the business manager expressed his experience of the event. He said, "I was sitting there with my back to you and heard you getting angry. I said to myself, "Wow, is Patrick losing it?" Then I turned around and saw that your body language was completely relaxed. I realized you weren't out of control but were *choosing* to express anger."

His interpretation was right on. I was consciously choosing to use anger as a tool to move toward resolution. Had I *reacted* from anger, we might not have come to a point of agreement, and it could have destroyed a business relationship (in which case, I would have learned another valuable lesson). As it was, we continued to do business with the printer, became closer, and in fact I presided over his memorial after his death the following year.

Believe me, I am not a master at this practice and do have moments when my emotions are reactive. But each time we choose our response, we strengthen our ability to respond from a higher place, from a place of soul potential. The power and importance of communication in directing emotions cannot be underestimated. We can direct our emotion in healthy ways through effective communication. We can also create healthy boundaries by communicating our needs and limits to those we encounter in all aspects of life, whether they are close relationships or brief encounters.

If we are angry or hurt, we can express those emotions in non-confronting ways. In doing so, we may not be expressing the full passion of our emotion, but that may not be necessary. Expressing our emotion calmly may be enough to avoid repression, and it will also have a more positive effect on the relationship.

It is always helpful to express yourself in a nonconfronting style—one that takes responsibility for your feelings. We all have experienced the difference in quality of expression when someone says something to us like, "I hate what you are doing to me," compared to, "My feelings are hurt by what you are doing." As mentioned earlier, when we express from our vulnerability, which means we are accessing deeper feelings, we draw people to us with compassion rather than creating distance and defensiveness by attacking.

We can also resolve conflict by communicating *nonverbally* in an effective way. If you find yourself in a situation that you cannot seem to resolve through dialogue, it is likely that you are too invested in *your* agenda to see into the heart of the other person involved. The old technique of putting yourself in someone else's shoes is a useful and powerful strategy. Put yourself in the other person's position and imagine how they might feel.

Sometimes this strategy is difficult, because you may not feel the way the other person does in that situation. If this is the case, try the exercise below to develop compassion and create a deeper understanding of the person with whom you are in conflict. It should be discussed at the outset that the goal of the exercise is not to get resolution or to fix the situation, although that may be a by-product. If you go into problem solving too soon, which is often the tendency, it will take you out of your feelings and into your head. The goal is to develop a deep level of empathy and understanding of the other person's feelings. From the deeper closeness that is achieved, solutions can be arrived at in a much easier and more magical way.

☀   ☀   ☀

Exercise for Understanding

Sit with the person whose feelings you wish to understand more deeply. Decide on the specific subject about which you are writing. Each of you will write down your feelings, taking responsibility for them. Stay with feelings and avoid statements that describe your partner or their behavior. Any statement where the word "feel" can be replaced with the word "think" is a thought not a feeling. For example, "I feel (think) you don't care about me" is not a feeling. "I feel hurt and unloved when you seem distant to me" is a feeling. Write as many examples you can think of. "I feel hurt and alone, like the time I got lost from my mother when I was five and I couldn't find her. I thought I was abandoned and would never see her again. I am afraid I will lose you."

After you each have finished writing, exchange papers and read what the other has written. When you are reading about your partner's feelings, think of times you have had similar feelings.

When each of you has finished reading, decide who will address the other's feelings first. As you are addressing the written material, ask questions to further understand the feelings of your partner and relate them to your own experience. Search for feelings you have had that relate to your partner's feelings and express them. "So you feel abandoned when I am in a quiet mood? I guess that is like how I felt when my mother would get mad at me and not speak to me. That was a terrible feeling. I didn't know my actions made you feel that way." When one partner feels that they have an understanding and empathy for the other, switch roles. Remember to avoid discussing resolutions until each one has developed the deeper understanding.

Quite often I have found that the feelings I had around the conflict were almost exactly the same as my partner's. Once this is realized, compassion takes over, and resolution is imminent.

❊   ❊   ❊

TRANSPERSONAL PSYCHOLOGY

Another way to heal and release emotional blocks is through transpersonal therapy. Most spiritual disciplines focus on the soul, the higher self, which is tied into our potential, our future. They often tell us to ignore the content of the lower unconscious or the shadow-self, which holds repressed emotion from the past. Looking to the light, to the potential, is a helpful step along the path, but it can be incomplete if there is a lot of emotional conflict from the lower unconscious that keeps pulling us into struggle.

Most psychological systems deal primarily with the lower unconscious. Traditional psychoanalysis generally spends years uncovering the conditioning elements from childhood. This is helpful also as it brings understanding to the patterns of our unconscious behavior. But without turning the attention to the soul and the potential, it can be a slow process. What we need most when we uncover unhealed emotional patterns is the light and love of our soul to heal them.

A seeker could practice both systems at once, getting the best of both worlds. But this might be difficult, as spiritual and psychological schools often contradict each other. Psychosynthesis is a form of transpersonal therapy designed to bring the best of spiritual practice and psychological therapy into one system. It uses imagery, psychodrama, and more traditional therapy to delve into the lower unconscious bringing up unhealed material from the past. At the same time, it uses imagery, meditation, affirmation, and behavior modification to access and integrate the light of the soul, or higher self, with the darkness of the shadow.

Psychosynthesis is a transpersonal therapy developed by Roberto Assagioli, who was a contemporary of Freud. He was not only a brilliant psychiatrist but also studied many mystical approaches. More than any other in his field at the time, he integrated or synthesized spirituality with the therapeutic process. He writes in *Psychosynthesis*, "We are dominated by everything with which our self becomes identified. We can dominate and control everything from which we disidentify ourselves."[4]

For example, any time we are identified as a hurt child, we will be controlled by the needs of that hurt child. If we are identified with being sick, we will be controlled by our sickness. When we are identified as a critical parent, we will be controlled by the needs of that subpersonality. Disidentifying from the subpersonality and identifying with the self allows us to choose how we want to direct that energy.

The exercise below is a simple model that can be used to identify and begin to heal patterns from the lower unconscious. It is usually much more effective to use such a technique with the assistance of a guide. We can generally go deeper into the lower unconscious when we are not in control of the process ourselves. The exercise is provided on the CD so that I can guide you to some degree. But real-ize that because I am not there with you to respond to your answers and help you direct your individual imagery, it may be a less com-plete process than if you were in the presence of a guide. Nevertheless, this can give you an idea of the process, open you to some new insights, and provide you with some helpful tools to heal unresolved emotional issues.

If you find that some emotions come up that are difficult for you to process or if you would like to explore the process at a deeper level, find yourself a qualified guide. Every human being can benefit from good emotional therapy. It can be difficult (or at least slower) to grow through emotional blocks without the assistance of outside guidance. The secret is finding the right guide—a therapist or spiri-tual teacher. I found my most recent guide by defining exactly what I wanted in a therapist and asking my angels to help me find him. The first person I contacted was the perfect person—an older, wiser version of myself who was a humanistic psychologist (versed in the teachings of Carl Rogers) and knowledgeable in psychosynthesis and other dynamic systems. He would guide me in precisely the way I would guide myself but with greater objectivity (which is the chief value of a guide), as he was, of course, outside of my psyche.

Before making an appointment with a therapist, don't be shy about inquiring about the methods or techniques that are used in their therapeutic system or what schools in which they studied. In addition to psychosynthesis, there are other schools that use transpersonal tech-niques, including Jungian, humanistic, and transactional psychology.

If you have an ability for self-exploration, you may have extraordinary results even without a guide. Give yourself about an hour of time for this process. It is possible that the exercise may bring up realizations that could be uncomfortable for you. If you do come across feelings that are more than you can sort out on your own, seek the assistance of a professional, preferably one who is experienced in working with imagery, so you can resolve whatever experiences you encounter.

❋   ❋   ❋

Exercise for Healing
Emotional Patterns
(Track 8 on Audio CD)

Receive an image of how you would like your life to be. Breathe in the feeling from that image. What within you might be keeping you from achieving that ideal? Receive an image of the emotional pattern. Give this image a name. Call it by its name and ask it why it is there. Ask it what is the beneficial reason for its existence. What did it protect you from when you were young? What is it protecting you from now? What does it need to be healed?

Become the image. Change places with it physically so you are sitting or standing where you imagine the image to be. What does it feel like to be the image? Let the emotion come as you answer your own questions. Why are you there? What do you need? If you feel anger, let it come. If it is pain, let yourself cry. Where is the tension in your body? Press that spot and release the tension. Let all the emotion that is stored there flow. Let it go. It has been there too long.

Take as much time as you need to let the emotion out.

As the image, tell yourself what you need to be healed. Ask for it. Become yourself again, looking at your image. What do you want to say to it? What do you want to do in the future to take responsibility for it, to heal it? Tell it what you will do. Ask it what its positive qualities are. How can you utilize its positive qualities? How can you direct this energy to protect you in healthy ways?

Get an image of a wise and perfect being. It could be a saint or sage. It could be an historical figure. It could be someone you know. It could be an abstract image that you have never seen before. . . . Ask it to give you advice on how to heal the image of your repressed emotions. Ask it to help you heal the energy.

Ask your wise being what you can do to help you remember this exercise and bring forth the images that have come from your own soul to empower you toward healing and fulfillment when situations come up that stimulate this emotional pattern.

❈   ❈   ❈

After completing the exercise, think about how you can apply what you have learned from it in your daily life. We can greatly advance our expression of the magic of the soul by honoring our feeling nature and directing it toward ever higher expressions of our ideal self.

Love your hatred.
Caress your pain.
Feel the power in your anger,
and focus it for good.
Allow your fear to inspire you to action.

7

The Magic of Sensation

✸ ✸ ✸

Observe Your Body

For free audio version, http://www.livingpurposeinstitute.com/meditation.htm

Observe your body. Where do you notice tension? Breathe deeply into those places. Notice how you can choose to relax your body. Observe the strength of your body. Recognize its incredible capacity to heal almost any illness. Do you know that ninety-seven percent of all illness can be healed by the body's natural process? Notice how you can train and condition your body to do incredible feats if you so choose. Appreciate how your body responds to love and nurturing. Appreciate the magical construct of your body. Recognize that you can choose what kind of body you want by how you treat and condition it.

Affirm that you have a body and yet you are more than your body.

How do you choose to be in your body?

✸ ✸ ✸

If you could clearly view the effects of your emotions, thoughts, the stresses you allow in your life, and the substances you put in your body on a day-to-day (or minute-to-minute) basis, how would you care for your body differently? If you loved yourself as much as you possibly could, how would you treat your body differently? We can greatly increase our ability to perform magic by purifying and conditioning our bodies, surrounding them with nature, using them as teachers by being present to their subtle messages, and freeing and enlightening our sexual energy.

Everything that has been offered about the magic of the soul in this book can be practiced without giving much attention to the body. But the effectiveness of the practice will be greatly influenced by the quality of the physical instrument (the body) used to implement the practice. If the body is filled with toxins from an unhealthy diet or is weak from stress, it will be much more difficult to receive and radiate light; to create fulfillment for ourselves and others. It is even difficult (but certainly not impossible) to have a positive outlook when the body is stressed, weak, or sick. Practicing the magic of the soul will lead to a healthier body. As we access the power of our souls more and more frequently, everything that stands in the way of a healthier and more complete expression of the soul is subject to purification.

I was not born with as strong a body as most people. I have a rare genetic disease called alpha 1 antitripsin deficiency, which can lead to various health challenges and was a significant factor (along with emotional stress factors) in my long-term illness mentioned earlier. I have been challenged with respiratory problems all of my life. While there have been many times that I have suffered as a result of my limitations, I have also learned to see the blessings in my weaknesses. It has been necessary for me to take care of my body with a greater diligence than most to enjoy the level of health that others have with less effort. Perhaps my soul chose this body so I would learn the value of a purified body. I heavily smoked, drank, and experimented with drugs in my youth, but it became clear quite quickly that I probably wouldn't live very long if I kept up those habits. As a result, I dropped my unhealthy ways and have been vigilant about eating a healthy diet, one that is free of sugar and flour with a high percentage of whole foods. I also use organic gardening to grow my own vegetables and fruits because even the organic food in health food stores contains about forty percent fewer vitamins than foods grown in uncultivated soil.

I want to be clear that I am not against the substances I list above from a moral perspective. No substance in itself is bad, it is only in how the substance is used that makes it healthy or unhealthy. Psychotropic drugs are used in spiritual ceremonies to reach higher levels of awareness, and other drugs are used for healing. Drugs can also be used to escape one's feelings or numb the consciousness. Tobacco is used both as a sacred herb in Native American customs, and is heavily abused in western cultures.

I have also been inspired to exercise regularly to keep my body as vibrant as possible. All of these practices have developed a body that is receptive to higher energies and spiritual influences. You too can increase your ability to manifest the magic of your soul by choosing to support your body in the healthiest ways possible. It is not necessary to have a physical weakness or disability to choose a purified vessel. It is difficult to do in our culture, however, because unhealthy habits are the norm.

I recommend treating your body as you would a brand new car that you love more than any you have ever owned. You would naturally buy a high-grade fuel for it and have it serviced regularly. You would clean it and groom it often to allow its beauty to shine to all the world.

Jesus Christ said the body is a temple. Imagine actually treating your body as a temple. Each time you begin to put something into your mouth, ask yourself the question, is this going to make my body healthier or weaker? Will this action increase or decrease my ability to share the light of my soul with others? Sometimes you may choose to make it weaker just because you know how good that chocolate cake will taste, but perhaps you will choose something healthier fifty or seventy-five percent of the time. Imagine how much healthier you would be.

Treat your body as a temple.

Many people don't know the benefits of a healthy diet because they have been eating and drinking high levels of sugar and processed foods since they were children. They have never detoxified, and so they have no idea how much more physical energy and clarity of mind they could enjoy by eliminating such detrimental substances. Many depend on caffeine for energy in the morning and then liquor to wind down at night. These are drugs, and their use over long periods of time takes its toll on the body and limits the body's ability to contact and radiate energy of a subtle, spiritual nature.

EXERCISING WITH MAGIC

Everything we do can be a meditation, which is expanded upon in the next chapter. Any physical exercise you perform can be performed in a way that inspires you to a meditative state. The natural endorphins released during exercise greatly facilitate the meditative state. Many athletes experience an altered state at various moments while performing their skills. The "runner's high" or "runner's zone" are common terms that describe the state of mind that long-distance runners commonly reach. The state is described as one where everything seems to be moving in slow motion. Every detail of every sight, sound, and smell is magnified and detailed.

Although this state is more common in long-distance running because of the intense physical exertion and the fact that it requires little use of the mind, it has also been described by athletes in almost all sports. I have heard many basketball players after their highest scoring games say, "I was in the zone. The basketball hoop looked so large that I couldn't miss it." Tennis players after their greatest matches have said that the tennis ball looked as large as a basketball. Baseball players have said that they could see the ball moving in slow motion into their mitt, or the pitch moving in slow motion before they hit it out of the park.

Usually these states happen spontaneously and infrequently. When I was a tennis pro, I developed a method for training the body and mind to move into the zone about which many athletes have spoken. The exercise below, which is based on Zen meditation, can be adapted to any sport or activity. In Zen meditation the goal is not to isolate the mind from the distractions in the environment but to expand the mind to include everything in the environment. I find this exercise works especially well in tennis because of the natural rhythm of the ball moving back and forth. It is much like the process of breathing. Hitting the ball is like the exhalation, and preparing to receive the ball is like the inhalation.

☀ ☀ ☀

Zen Tennis Exercise

Begin by being aware of your body as you are playing. Notice your breathing and the movements of your body. Watch the ball closely as it leaves your opponent's racket. Watch it coming over the net intently. Watch the rotation of the ball as it comes off the bounce all the way up to your strings. (This will improve your game if you only go this far. Most people don't watch the ball hit their strings.)

Continue to do this until it becomes natural. Now, expand your awareness to include watching not only the ball with complete attention but also the area around the ball. See the lines or cracks on the court as the ball comes up to your strings. See the details of the net as the ball crosses it but don't decrease your focus on the ball. Gradually, continue to expand your awareness of your environment to include the clothing of your opponent, the fence around the court, the sights and sounds around the court, any aroma in the air. Allow yourself to be completely one with the total experience in the moment.

☀ ☀ ☀

You can adapt this exercise to any sport or activity. Just focus on the most central aspect of the task and allow the awareness to gradually move outward until it envelops the total experience of what you are doing. Most people find this process easy and get into the zone quite effortlessly. When I have success in tennis lessons with this exercise, students begin to apply all of the techniques I have been teaching them without thinking about it. Once I sense a student is in the zone, I don't say anything. No instruction is needed at that point. There is a time for structured learning and a time for surrendering so that the structured learning can manifest in a nonstructured experience in the ever present now. Some people don't achieve a complete meditative state, but the mere act of watching the ball and being more aware of the tennis experience increases their ability in the moment.

When I am in the zone, I automatically turn over trust to my body. I no longer tell it what to do but allow it to perform the way it organically knows how. Another by-product of being in the zone is that my body knows its limit. If I am playing from a perspective of wanting to win, I will often go for the big shot; sometimes, it even works. If I am in the zone, I don't do more than what my body knows it can do or needs to do to be one with the activity. My hitting becomes more consistent, more rhythmic, and by the way, I could care less about winning. The joy of being completely and totally in the bliss of the moment is far greater than any win. In fact, nonattachment is a by-product and a prerequisite for being in the zone whether we are involved in exercise, other activities, or the achievement of an important goal. The funny thing is that the likelihood of winning while in the zone is higher because we perform better when there is no attachment to winning: There is also no fear of losing. Most missed shots in tennis are a result of the fear of missing. Most missed opportunities in life are a result of the fear of failure.

CONNECTION WITH NATURE

Much of our modern-day illness and phobia can be traced to a societal loss of contact with nature. Clearly, there is more crime and mental illness in regions of higher industrialization than in rural areas. Living in the country is a slower, more relaxed, and certainly healthier environment than the city. This is due in part to the larger numbers of people but also to the lack of contact with nature. There are many advantages to living in the city, but among the disadvantages are the health detriments that result from less contact with nature.

The more cement that surrounds us, the less nature we have contact with. The human body and psyche need nature, plants, earth, and clear sky to thrive. There is an old saying by native peoples: "Do not live where the hawks no longer fly, for these are places of disease and death."

If you are a camper, you have probably noticed that when camping, people in other campsites are usually very friendly. Is this because people are happy that they are away from their jobs? Perhaps in part, but I also think it is because there are less apparent boundaries between ourselves and nature and each other. While camping, we often cook and eat outside the place where we sleep. This is exactly how it works in tribal cultures. I bet that if we all lived in tents or tepees, we would know our neighbors much better than we do living in houses and working in buildings.

I am fortunate to live in an area that is close to the culture of the city and yet has a very natural setting. Our house is also at the end of a cul-de-sac, so children can play in the street safely. Parents often play outside with children or talk to other neighbors as part of the outdoor community. It is the friendliest neighborhood in which I have ever lived. And yes, the hawks still fly here. In fact, the last three locations in which I have lived were abundant in hawks and other wildlife. This is one of the criteria I use to select a home.

When I conducted a *Primal Fire Intensive*, which was a campout workshop that I held in the Angeles National Forest about nine years ago, my intent was to inspire a peak experience of each participant's primal self. There was no philosophical theory presented, only exercises designed to remind the participants of the natural self.

I did not define the primal self based on any preconceived idea. The purpose was for each person to find out who their true self was when they were taken out of the context of their normal lives and societal rules and conventions. While the intensive achieved its purpose, another interesting result emerged that I hadn't intended.

The most profound result of the encounter was the degree of community that was created within one day of the training. There was a group cooking area, where everyone prepared food and ate together. As people prepared food, they offered it to others, and the entire process became a group effort. I had never experienced a group that bonded as quickly as this one. I concluded that at the level of our primal origins, we are a species that needs and thrives in an environment of community, and we become connected through nature. Houses and cement separate us from nature and from each other. I am not suggesting that we deconstruct our modern civilization, but that we augment our living to allow for as much nature and community as possible for the sake of our health and well-being.

If you live in a densely populated city, surround yourself and your home with as much plant life as you can. Make frequent trips to nature for vacation or even day outings. It is amazing how much perspective we can gain by spending a day by a river or on a mountaintop.

In the last few years, I have added sabbaticals to my regular camping trips, where I camp alone for a few days. There is nothing that gives me more peace and a sense of my true self than being alone in nature. The importance of communing with nature is exemplified in this excerpt from an essay on "Nature" by Emerson.

all the "stuff" you have to do

At the gates of the forest, the surprised man of the world is forced to leave his city estimates of great and small, wise and foolish. The knapsack of custom falls off his back with the first step he makes into these precincts. Here is sanctity which shames our religions, and reality which discredits our heroes. Here we find nature to be the circumstance which dwarfs every other circumstance, and judges like a god all men that come to her. We have crept out of our

✓ *all nature — no judgement*

close and crowded houses into the night and morning, and we see what majestic beauties daily wrap us in their bosom.[1]

The Body as Teacher

The body is the most efficient biofeedback device ever developed, but we often forget to use it. We may ignore that subtle tightness in our stomach that indicates we are acting in a way that is causing us stress. We might try to fight off those butterflies that indicate we are afraid of something instead of facing the fear or an underlying issue that is causing it. We may take medication to relieve the head pain or indigestion that is telling us we need to relax.

When we live in the magic of the soul, we are present to what is happening in each moment. We are aware of everything in our environment as well as what is happening within our bodies, minds, and emotions even on subtle levels. We can practice this at any moment in time. As you are read these words, be aware of your environment. Be aware of the sights you can see with your peripheral vision and the sounds you can hear. Be aware of any aroma in the air. Most importantly, be aware of your self. What is going on in your feeling nature, in your mind, and in your physical body? Notice any tension that is being held. You don't have to analyze it. You can do that at some point if you wish, but for now, just be present to your total experience. Allow any awareness that comes up concerning the state of your being, but don't analyze it. Just be receptive to the information.

There are many systems of healing, personal growth, and spiritual awakening that utilize the body as an entry point into greater awareness. Vipassana Yoga is an ancient system that begins the investigation of self-awareness by stilling the mind and becoming aware of the body. The goal is to investigate all tensions and simply observe them and learn from them in a meditative state.

The following exercise can be used to create a greater awareness of your physical being and the subtle internal forces that influence it.

✺ ✺ ✺

Exercise for
Tuning in to Your Body
(Track 9 on Audio CD)

Sit in a comfortable position with your back straight. Breathe deeply and watch your breath as it draws inward, filling your lungs completely; watch as it is expelled completely. Breathe regularly and continue to watch your breath. Now be aware of the point between breaths—between inhaling and exhaling—exhaling and inhaling—the center between giving and receiving—outward focus and inward—yin and yang—spirit and earth—positive and negative—life and death. . . . Now be aware of other subtle areas of your physiology—your heartbeat, the blood circulating in your veins, the electrical communication within your nervous system. . . . Be aware of any tensions in your body. Just let them be there without judging them. Breathe deeply into the tension. Notice if your observation brings you clarity on how to live in a way that is healthier for your body. How can you eliminate tension through harmonious action? Take as much time as you need to address all aspects of your body that are out of harmony or holding energy. Breathe into each one of them until you find clarity and peace.

✺ ✺ ✺

IS SEX SPIRITUAL?

It is interesting to me that the question even needs to be asked. Why has sex been downplayed or even suppressed by various spiritual disciplines and most cultures throughout history? Although mankind has evolved to a more complex state of emotional, mental, and spiritual development than that of the animal kingdom, we too still possess animal drives. Our animal drives, such as aggressiveness and sexuality, have in the past, and in many cases in the present, tended to overpower mental and spiritual values. The moral values of individuals have in many cases been cast aside by overpowering drives such as lust. Many systems advise transcending the physical in order to ascend in awareness to the spiritual. Historically, it was easier to embrace spiritual values and energy by ignoring, suppressing, or depreciating physical needs. But the suppression of any natural drive can have unhealthy consequences. As needs are suppressed, they usually become stronger and, in many cases, lead to perversion or illness.

At some point, each individual (and humanity as a whole) will evolve enough to integrate the two great opposing forces: spirit and matter, soul and body. In the past, the spiritual goal has been to raise the kundalini (life force energy) up the spine and into the head—the connection with the spiritual. The goal for many and the future for everyone is to bring the energy from spirit down into the body, to descend heaven unto earth. As mentioned previously in relation to the soul, we strive for spirit by reaching for the soul. When we reach the soul, we turn our attention to the personality. We focus spiritual values through soul intent into the physical plane. Being an ascetic has had its value and place, but the ultimate goal is to become the magician of the soul who blends spirit with form. This is the magic of being human. It is our challenge and our mission to fuse spirit into matter. Sexuality and creativity are the same energy, expressed through different streams of consciousness.

---

*Honor your sexuality as something sacred
and your passion will become spiritual
and your spirituality will become passionate.*

Truth lies at the center of two opposing ideas. The answer is never one nor the other, but some combination of both. The tension between two opposites is sexuality birthing new life. How do you feel about your sexuality? Do you feel it is spiritual?

God is Sex.

God is the Creative Principle in its purest form. The drawing together of two individuals out of love or even erotic desire is God's creativity at work. Imagine the power of the purest form of spiritual force perfectly blended with the most vibrant of physical energy—blending these two is the magical purpose of being human.

What would it be like if you could see your most erotic fantasy as an expression of God's love?

I realize this may be a challenging idea for many. Even those who find it acceptable and healthy as an idea may find it hard to accept emotionally. Our culture has a long-standing belief system about sexuality being, at minimum, nonspiritual and, at the extreme, evil. Like any belief system, it holds our reality in place. It took years for me to let go of the programming that shaped my own sexual repression. Imagine the freedom of recognizing completely that healthy sexual expression and fantasy is a beautiful part of being human?

How do we make our sexuality spiritual and our spirituality more vibrantly creative? Most people separate the two. What is done in the bedroom is far removed from anything spiritual. And to speak of spirituality and sexuality in the same breath is blasphemy. When you think about it, isn't such a division ludicrous? Sexuality is what creates new life. When we are involved in intercourse we are closer to God than at any other time because we are engaged in an act that

could potentially bring a new being into life. What could be more
sacred? In addition, the moments leading up to and through orgasm
are when we are most able to lose our self-identity and merge with
another being, perhaps all beings and all life. When I experience
orgasm as an expression of deep love, I am no longer me. I become
life itself, completely divorced from my mind and alive with sensory experience in the here and now. I lose all sense of self in that
moment. The description of the psychological experience of orgasm
(not the physical description) could be easily transposed as an
account of mystical experience.

So spirituality is inherent in the sexual act. Like anything else,
though, we can pervert sexuality. Because our society has come so
far from its natural roots, perversion in all areas is rampant. But we
can reclaim our nature by consciously integrating our spirituality
with our sexuality. We can see any nonviolent sexual act as an act of
spirit. If that act does not fit into our idea of spirituality, we can either
widen that idea (because it is too narrow) or direct our sexual activities in healthier directions (because they are not healthy enough to
fit into a balanced spiritual ideal). The intent of bringing these two
opposites together will lead us to a healthier pursuit of both ends of
the polarity.

If we feel our spirituality is not vibrant, it is probably lacking
creativity, which is sexuality at a higher level. If we accept a teaching because it is written in scripture or because someone else has
said it is so, we may find that it isn't challenging us to use our God-
given abilities to discover spiritual truth for ourselves. If our spiritual practice is rote and has little meaning in the moment, it will most
likely not be fulfilling. Engage your creativity in your spiritual practice. Find new ways of applying your spirituality through your work,
your relationships, your thoughts, feelings, words, and actions.

Conceive and give birth
to a vibrant celebration of Spirit.

The previous three chapters have focused on the personality and its expression of soul force in the world of form. When the body is relatively purified of toxins and stress—the emotions are clear and the mind is still—there is no alternative but to experience absolute bliss. This is the natural state of spiritual energy, which is what we are made of. When we recognize that we are more than our sensations, feelings, and thoughts, more than our perceptions in the world of form, we become immersed in this profound experience of the ecstasy of being alive, of being one with all life, of being.

For a powerful audio version of the disidentification exercise, which combines the opening exericises at the beginning of these last three chapters, please visit www.livingpurposeinstitute.com/meditation.htm

8

Meditation

Meditation is the foundation upon which the practice of the magic of the soul rests. As I mentioned earlier, prayer is the act of talking to God, and meditation is the act of listening. Both are important, but since God has more to offer than we do as an individualized identification of God, listening is good advice. The exercises throughout this book and the practice of the magic of the soul are all forms of meditation. Meditation opens us to the pulse of our soul and also provides a method for that pulse to sound forth as a rhythmic beat in the world of practical application.

There are many different types of meditation and thousands of books written on the subject, so I will not go into detail about various systems. I will provide some of the basic understandings at which I have arrived and some specific applications that have been less publicized, including meditating as a service, dreaming as a meditation, and ceremony.

Meditation has been defined in many different ways. I like to think of it as a natural process, one that does not necessarily require a ritual (like sitting in a particular position or chanting or breathing, although all of these techniques are helpful). Meditation is a way of piercing the veil of sensory illusion, and it can be done anywhere and at any moment.

There are many more people who have tried meditation in some form or another who don't meditate on a regular basis than there are people who have made it a consistent practice. Why is this? A common comment by those who have meditated for many years is that the benefits are so subtle and occur so gradually that you don't fully recognize them until after years of practice. There are some benefits you may never fully realize as having come directly from meditation. I don't know exactly how much of my growth over the years has been a result of meditation or of just learning from life's experiences. But I am certain that my growth has been *at least* tenfold what it would have been had I not been meditating consistently for the last twenty-seven years. I am speaking of spiritual and emotional growth but also my ability to focus and direct my mind as well as achieve goals and success.

Years ago, when I was asked in a television interview what I got out of meditating, I remember answering that "it is easier to explain what I miss when I don't meditate. I gradually forget about the peace, the centeredness, the focus that I enjoy when I meditate regularly. Once I get back to meditating consistently, I remember." Meditation is a process of remembering who I truly am at a deep level. Now, I can't even imagine life without meditation. It seems the further I have progressed along my spiritual path, the more self-understanding I have gained that I can lose sight of or forget about that consistent meditation reinforces for me. Not that I lose it completely, but meditating each day reinforces and adds to the ongoing practice of self-directed spiritual evolution.

We can meditate while we are walking down the street, exercising, or even talking during conversation. Those enlightened beings who have mastered the meditative process live life as a grand meditation. The morning meditation can be a way of affirming a meditative state for the entire day. Each morning in meditation, I not only become still and at peace in the moment, but I create a vibration that I seek to maintain throughout the entire day.

---

*Meditate to receive and radiate
light on a consistent basis.*

Each morning, commit to represent and share the energy of your highest self, your soul, throughout the day (even if you only spend fifteen seconds in quiet meditation, it can make a difference).

RECEPTIVE AND CREATIVE MEDITATION

I divide the various meditative processes into two basic forms: creative and receptive meditation. Creative meditation can consist of any type of guided imagery or mental focus that creates an altered state of consciousness that is conducive to inner discovery or growth. Receptive meditation is the act of transcending the thought process completely, stilling the rational mind, and experiencing a quality of consciousness more subtle than thought. It is through this latter process that many have received the gift of mystical experience, or even cosmic consciousness.

Most of the exercises in this book are examples of creative meditation. They are designed to arrive at a particular state or insight or to achieve a goal. Many traditional paths would not consider these meditations at all and would only consider what I am calling receptive meditation as true meditation. But I believe that any technique that furthers your experience, understanding, or expression of soul, which includes all conscious growth, is an act of meditation.

Ultimately, most meditators practice a combination of creative and receptive meditation. Even simple methods of watching the breath or chanting can be considered forms of creative meditation designed to lead the meditator into a state of receptive meditation. My own meditation form changes as I grow and become interested in different areas of spiritual growth. Lately, my form includes simply stilling the mind. Sometimes, I will use chanting to achieve this and other times I will simply become aware of myself as the energy of all life by letting go of my mental process and my self-identity. I frequently use imagery to focus on a particular goal that I am manifesting using an adaptation of Exercise for Creating Magic in chapter 3. I always finish with sending light and love to specific individuals and to the world.

Using imagery in creative meditation to accomplish what you want in life is a well-tested and effective strategy. Anything that is accomplished begins as an image in the mind. In fact, if you accomplish anything that isn't an accident (if there is such a thing), you first must have an image. The clearer the image, the easier it is to accomplish the goal and the greater will be the quality of the accomplishment. Whenever I began teaching tennis to a new student, I emphasized that the best practice they could do in the first couple of weeks was mental practice. I would ask them to visualize themselves practicing their newly learned strokes in their mind's eye. You would be amazed at the startling difference between those students who took my advice and those who didn't. Not only did they learn more quickly, but they would generally end up with much better form in the long run.

Various studies have shown that people who practice any sport using visualization will improve more than if they don't practice at all and, in some cases, more than if they practice only physically. Michael Jordan cited his natural ability to visualize as a contributor to his unprecedented success in basketball in his book, *For the Love of the Game*.

> I have used visualization techniques for as long as I can remember. I always visualized my success. It wasn't until later in my career that I realized the technique is something that most people have to learn. I had been practicing the principles naturally my entire life. I visualized how many points I was going to score, how I was going to score them, how I was going to break down my opponent.[1]

His uncanny natural ability is likely a major reason for his tremendous success in becoming perhaps the greatest professional basketball player ever and possibly the greatest professional athlete ever—certainly the most celebrated.

Try using visualization to improve anything you wish to learn or achieve. Simply close your eyes and imagine yourself performing the task perfectly, effortlessly. People who are not naturally visual can be successful at this technique. If you struggle at *seeing* the images internally, it just means that you are probably more auditory or kinesthetic in how you process information. In this case, try adding the sounds that would represent the perfect, effortless accomplishment to the internal experience. Try *feeling* what it would be like to accomplish the goal or activity perfectly and effortlessly. During your visualizations, affirm that you are performing the task in the present moment in your mind. In other words, rather than projecting the image into the future, imagine that you are doing the task in the now. The Exercise for Accomplishing Goals in chapter 1 is a good example of how to use visualization for the purpose of actualization.

Creative meditation is how many people begin, because it is easier. It is easier to follow imagery to a peaceful state, a new insight, or a specific goal than it is to simply stop the mind, which is one aim of all receptive meditation. It sounds like a simple task, but if you don't have experience with receptive meditation (or even if you have but want to test yourself), stop reading at the end of this paragraph, look at your watch, and still your mind. Close your eyes and see if you can go one minute without thinking a single thought.

If you succeeded and have never practiced this before, then you probably have the potential to become the greatest sage the world has ever known. The difficulty in stilling the mind is a common reason why many beginning meditators give up. Isn't it ironic that the most difficult thing for a human being to do is nothing?

One definition of receptive meditation is simply the act of letting go. While there are varied techniques to assist in this process, ultimately the goal is to transcend even the process. Even to say that there is a goal is misleading, because when we arrive at the center of our spiritual self, we realize that it's not a place to get to but a state of being that was there all along. To experience that state, we need to let go. Let go of the goal, let go of striving to realize soul awareness, and you are there. It's all about surrender and, ultimately, doesn't require a process, but as I mentioned earlier about spiritual awakening, it seems that everyone who arrives at that state and later communicates how they got there used a process to recognize that they didn't need a process.

The goal of the two exercises on stilling the mind in chapter 5,

The Magic of Thought, is to reach a state of receptive meditation. The technique of imagining the consciousness becoming lighter is a method that I developed to reach beyond the realm of mind. I have had profound experiences using this technique. Other techniques include watching the breath until the mind quiets, which is widely used in Buddhist practices. Chanting is a common and effective technique prevalent in indigenous and eastern traditions (it is quite prevalent in Hinduism) and even in traditional western religions as well. Gregorian chanting is one of the most beautiful expressions of spiritual singing. There are also open-eyed meditations such as the Taoist technique of staring at a point on a wall or off in the distance. Another is watching a candle flame. Staring at a mandala is a very common eastern practice as well.

Yoga is an ancient practice associated with Hinduism that combines specific postures that exercise the body and at the same time inspire a meditative state. The exercises are not only healthy for the body but are helpful in clearing the mind and raising the consciousness to a higher level. Tai chi is used by Buddhists and Taoists and employs slow and methodical martial arts movements to discipline the body and mind together.

As I mentioned in the previous chapter, I have found Zen Buddhist meditation to be quite helpful in its application to sports. In Zen meditation, rather than trying to isolate consciousness and still the mind by eliminating sights, sounds, and thoughts from the mind, the technique is inclusive. While you are reading this passage, be aware of your body, heartbeat, and breath. Be aware of your surroundings, including any subtle sounds that may be present in your environment. The Zen technique is designed to bring you into a more present state and, ultimately, one that connects you with all life. A meditative state is less a place we get to than simply a process of becoming more aware of where we are. It isn't out there, it is in here, right where we are. We can be present not only to our physical environment but to our own feelings at a deep level, to the inner workings of our psyche, and, ultimately, to the subtle vibration of the divine that exists in everyone and everything.

Be one with all life right now.

I recommend trying all of the receptive meditation techniques listed above. Meditating in a group is easier for everyone I have ever heard comment on the subject. Because we are connected in mind and energy, when we meditate with others, we are affected by the success of others meditating in the group. If you are fortunate to find a group that has very experienced meditators, your progress can be dramatically enhanced. The heightened states you achieve in the group meditation can then be aspired to and integrated in individual meditation. Often after meditating in a group, I find my individual meditations reach a higher level.

MEDITATION AS A SERVICE

Meditation as a service can combine creative and receptive meditation. The meditator often uses some form of visualization to connect with spiritual force and then simply becomes receptive to the flow of spiritual energy. The intent is to create a positive force of peace and goodwill in the world during the meditation and also to reinforce a consistent radiation of positive energy on an ongoing basis.

You can practice meditation as a service on your own in your personal meditation. Each day when I meditate, part of my meditation includes allowing light to flow through me to all of my loved ones, to those for whom I have agreed to pray, and finally, to the entire world. As an affirmation, I try to radiate that experience throughout the day as often as I can.

Receive light by stretching your consciousness upward and outward on a regular basis. Breathe in soul light through the top of your head. Breathe in vitality from the earth through the soles of your feet. Blend the energies of spirit and matter with the energy of your heart and let it flow outward.

Practice radiating light from your heart while you are doing your job—in a hospital—lying in bed before you go to sleep—driving on the freeway—playing tennis—playing golf—feeling frightened, hurt, or angry—meeting with your boss—doing your homework—making love—writing a book—dying.

Meditation for Radiating Light

For free audio version, http://www.livingpurposeinstitute.com/meditation.htm

Close your eyes and use whatever technique best aligns you with your soul. Feel your awareness reaching into the earth and grounding you. Feel your awareness reaching to the heavens, expanding to receive spiritual light. Imagine light pouring through the top of your head and flowing out through your mind, heart, and hands. Imagine it flowing through you toward the images of people for whom you want to pray. Imagine it expanding outward in all directions, filling the room, moving beyond the walls of the room, stretching out across the city in which you live, expanding throughout your country, spreading over oceans and continents until it surrounds the entire planet. Remain a radiant point with light flowing through you as a positive force for the planet as long as it feels appropriate for you. When you have completed the radiation of light, think of ways you can radiate light in your life through your thoughts, feelings, words, and actions. Take a deep breath and open your eyes feeling better than ever.

Another way to meditate as a service that has even greater power is to link up with others who meditate or pray for the good of all. There are many organizations and movements that promote united prayer and meditation. For the past twenty years, I have observed a practice called Triangles. In this practice, you agree to link up once each day with two other people and visualize sending light to each other. You visualize a triangle of light connecting you with the other two. Then, you imagine a vast network of triangles surrounding the planet that is made up of others who are performing the same ritual. What is created is a web of light made up of a myriad of geometrical patterns formed by the network of triangles. Then you say a prayer of peace or spiritual invocation. Some people link up at a specified time and others do it whenever it is convenient, recognizing that time does not exist in the world of spiritual energy. The person who introduced this process to me, Jenilee Barnum, proposed the idea that because everyone links up at different times around the world, it is like a wave of interlinked light that blinks or fades in and out on a consistent basis over each twenty-four-hour period.

Triangles is a worldwide practice sponsored by the Arcane School in New York.[2] You can become a registered triangle or you can embark on your own. If you register, you will receive an inspirational monthly newsletter. You can also obtain copies of "The Great Invocation," a universal prayer that is recommended to be used with this service. The more people involved in this powerful practice, the more power and positive effect that can be achieved.

The World Peace Prayer Society[3] originated in Japan and has offices in several countries around the world. They promote world peace through encouraging people and groups to recite the simple prayer, "May peace prevail on Earth." This ceremony, which is performed by people around the world each day, consists of praying for each of the 191 countries of the world with the following words:

> *May peace prevail on Earth.*
> *May peace be in (name of country).*
> *May peace prevail on Earth.*

Reciting the prayer for each country creates a repetitive mantra while participants visualize peace going to each country prayed for. It takes about 40 minutes to complete the ceremony. Following is a message from Masami Sainji, the chairperson of the organization:

As we move forward into the twenty-first century we encourage all of you to take a positive step toward universal understanding. Touch people with the message of love. Pray for the peace and happiness of people in all other lands and cultures. Make a commitment to world peace by honoring the earth, honoring its people, and celebrating the unity of the human spirit.

World Healing Day 1986 was the first of an annual event inviting people of all faiths to meet in groups for the purpose of united prayer and meditation on December 31. In his book, *The Planetary Commission*, John Price proposed that everyone meet at the specifically designated time of noon Greenwich time. The idea was to create a meeting time when everyone participating would be connected in spiritual intent at the exact same moment. The first event drew millions of people to churches and meditation halls around the world. You can check local New Thought churches (Religious Science, Unity, etc.) to participate in this ongoing service.

Another worldwide practice is meditating at the time of the full moon as well as the equinoxes and solstices each year. People from all faiths and cultures join together in united prayer and meditation to receive and radiate spiritual energy to create a positive force of peace and goodwill throughout the planet. These ceremonies have their roots in ancient customs. To participate, check your local metaphysical bookstores for local groups or search the World Wide Web.

WHY MEDITATE AS A SERVICE?

What is the benefit of united meditation? Why is it different than meditating on my own? Does meditating for others or the world really have any effect? Numerous studies have proven that groups of individuals who prayed for sick people actually helped them recover faster than those who were not prayed for *even if the participants didn't know they were being prayed for*, ruling out a placebo effect.

One of the most quoted scientific studies of prayer was done between August 1982 and May 1983. Three hundred ninety-three patients in the San Francisco General Hospital's Coronary Care Unit participated in a double blind study to assess the therapeutic effects of prayer. Patients were randomly selected by computer to either receive or not receive prayer. All participants in the study, including patients, doctors, and the conductor of the study were not aware of which patients were being prayed for and which were not.

The patients who had received prayer as a part of the study turned out healthier than those who had not been prayed for. The prayed-for group had less need for CPR and less need for mechanical ventilators. They had a diminished necessity for diuretics and antibiotics, less occurrences of pulmonary edema, and fewer deaths.

In the 1970s, studies were conducted proving that the crime rate in cities dropped significantly when 1 percent of the population of the city was meditating on a regular basis. The subjects in the study were part of the Transcendental Meditation movement developed by Maharishi Mehesh Yogi in the 1950s.

In the initial study, conducted in 1972, eleven cities with populations larger than 25,000 were investigated.[4] These cities had reached 1 percent participation in the Transcendental Meditation program. The "1 percent" cities showed an average decrease in crime rate of 8.2 percent from 1972 to 1973, while the crime rate of the controlled cities increased on an average of 8.3 percent. Below are changes in crime rates for the cities studied.

Cities with 1% practicing TM		*Control Cities*	
City Name	*% Change*	*City Name*	*% Change*
Ames, IA	-3.6	Columbia, MO	+11.2
Bloomington, IN	-4.5	Costa Mesa, CA	-3.9
Boulder, CO	-9.1	Fort Collins, CO	-3.2
Carbondale, IL	-9.9	Lafayette, IN	+11.1
Chapel Hill, NC	-9.3	Marshalltown, IA	+5.0
Davis, CA	-15.2	Monterey, CA	+8.5
Iowa City, IW	-2.5	Norman, OK	+20.8
Ithaca, NY	-0.6	Oshkosh, WI	+8.3
Lawrence, KS	-18.4	Pleasant Hill, CA	-1.2
Santa Barbara, CA	-8.8	Poughkeepsie NY	+14.4
Santa Cruz, CA	-7.9	Rocky Mountain, NC	+20.2

These results are further evidence of the effects of the hundredth monkey syndrome (described in chapter 3). But meditators who have seriously practiced meditation as a world service don't need studies or theories to validate the effectiveness of the process. We feel the effects as we meditate. It is a reality that cannot be denied when it is practiced over time.

If people can be healed by others praying for them, and if 1 percent of the population of any area has the degree of success indicated in the study above, imagine the results if 5, 10, or 50 percent of the global population meditated for the well-being of the planet. If Rupert Sheldrake's theory of morphic resonance is valid (and I believe it is), imagine the morphic field created when millions of people put their minds together for a common purpose of creating peace and harmony. Clearly, war would be impossible if *everyone* meditated in this way. Jesus said that "where two or more are gathered in my name, I am there among them." The Christ consciousness—the consciousness of Universal Love—is present when any group of individuals comes together in united intent. The more people who gather, the greater the spiritual presence and the greater is our potential power for positive change.

So much of our world conflict is a result of focusing on our contrasting beliefs. The mind departmentalizes and separates. What unites us is our hearts. You can have a profound effect (even if you don't *see* the results in the world) by joining or starting a meditation or prayer group. It only takes two people to begin a group. For a generic all-denominational meditation format, go to www.spiritualunitymovement.org. You can also initiate such groups in your existing spiritual community. People everywhere are opening to the power of united spiritual service. You can make an enormous difference by adding your intention and service to the global effort.

DREAMING AS A MEDITATION

Just as we can live life consciously as a meditation, we also can live consciously in our dream life. In the Carlos Castaneda series, Don Juan emphasized the practice of lucid dreaming. Finally after years of instruction, Carlos had an experience of affecting reality from a dream state.[5] Don Juan commented afterward that Carlos may someday recognize that the dream body is the real body, and it is the body of our waking awareness that is the illusion. In embracing the world of our soul, we may find that our dreams are reality and our lives are but the dream of our soul.

We can practice living our lives as though they were dreams. If you don't like the way your dream is going, change it. You can dream whatever you want. There are no limitations in dreamtime. When you are faced with a challenge, ask yourself how you would change the reality if you were dreaming. By doing this, you can open your awareness, your mind, to a magical state. Look at every situation and every encounter as a fluid dream state—dream yourself to enlightenment.

Live your dream!

We can also treat our dreamtime as an objective reality. Affirm that you can alter your life through your dreams. Choose to be awake and alive in your dreams. This practice has profound implications. Buddhism teaches that the after-death state is much like a dream state. Imagine living in the hereafter as though it were a dream. The way the average person dreams, it would be very difficult to navigate through the afterlife state—to be conscious. As a metaphor, when we live our waking lives unconsciously we are asleep as well. One goal of Buddhist practice is to become awake while dreaming, so that when the afterlife comes, an ability to be conscious will already have been developed.

Lucid dreaming has had little exploration by the mainstream up to this point. The average person will require a great deal of practice to become proficient at this skill, but how many truly profound developmental steps can you take while you are asleep? It requires no extra time, and it is a virtually effortless practice. I have practiced this technique on and off over the years and have had some success at it. I know others who travel where they want every night. They visit those with whom they do business and prepare ahead in dream-time for important events to come. There were times when a magical teacher of mine, Ed Porrazzo, would show up in my dreams and the next day I would receive a phone call from him asking me if I received his message. Practicing lucid dreaming can be an easy and fun experience if you don't get caught up in results. The exercise below is an excellent introduction to this practice.

Exercise for Dreaming
(Track 10 on Audio CD)

While awake, ask yourself repeatedly throughout the day, "Am I dreaming?" Give yourself a cue, such as asking the question every time you walk through a doorway. Or ask the question every time you look at your watch. As much as possible, imagine that your waking life is like a dream.

Before you go to sleep, affirm that you wish to be awake in your dreams. Decide what you would like to dream. Take your consciousness there. When your waking-time cue comes up in a dream—you walk through a door-way—the question may automatically enter your dream, "Am I dreaming?" Seize the opportunity to recognize that you are and that you can be aware while you are in dreamtime.

Decide what you want to dream on a daily basis. Decide what goals you would like to accomplish through dreaming. Write down your dreams as soon as you wake up and keep a daily log. This will help bring your dream-state awareness into your daily consciousness. It will also inspire a higher level of dreaming as your unconscious mind recognizes your intent to learn from your dream experience.

CEREMONY

Every ceremony can be considered a form of meditation. Ceremony applies symbolism, the language of the soul, in physical form and is an essential element in human life. Being human means to be affected by ceremony and ritual. If we do not use healthy ritual, we will most likely be dominated by obsessive ritual.

For the most part, our culture has lost its appreciation for healthy ritual. As a result, our society has bred obsessive ritual. Most people wake and get ready for work the same way each day. They drive to the same place and perform the same duties over and over. Our lives can become rote with little creativity involved. We may even create destructive obsessive ritual, such as overeating, alcoholism, drug addiction, or sexual addiction, to help fill the void left by the absence of sacred ritual.

How can you create healthy ritual in your life through sacred ceremony? It need not be in a traditional way. In fact, ceremony is most empowering when it symbolizes what is happening in your heart. The most effective ritual is that which brings the greatest feeling.

Create a ceremony to make the morning sacred. It could be praying each morning, singing an inspirational song, meditating, or ringing a bell and listening to its sound slowly fade until it melts into silence. In each activity imagine that it is bringing you closer to the peace that you will feel throughout the day. Create an altar and gaze at it. Run before leaving for work and appreciate your body and nature as you breathe deeply from the exertion. Do yoga or tai chi. Or just breathe deeply, appreciating the good things in your life as well as the magical lessons you encounter each day.

Any action can be done ceremoniously. Life itself can be seen as one grand ceremony. Embracing such awareness inspires sure passage to the magic of the soul. Imagine going about daily tasks with the rhythm of spiritual ceremony dancing through your soul. Think of ways you can bring greater order and grace into your life through sacred ceremony.

If you attend a church, mosque, or temple, participate fully in the ceremony. When you design a ceremony for any rite of passage (wedding, divorce, funeral, birthday, entering into adulthood, sexual birth, childbirth), do so with the intent of releasing soul power. If it is a formal ceremony, don't leave the creativity to the person you have hired. Make it real for you.

I officiated the wedding of a couple who inspired me through designing their ceremonies with conscious intent. I also performed christenings for both of their children. For their wedding, they took a rose ceremony that I provided as part of my basic format and adapted it in a creative way. They arranged flowers into bouquets, each of different colors, to be offered by various members of their families. At one point during the ceremony, I invited the family members to bring the flowers to the outdoor altar. I named qualities (ascribed by the couple) that represented the colors and the energies of the seven chakras (energy centers) in the body and the seven rays that run through all life. Each family member carrying a group of flowers symbolically offered those qualities as gifts to the ceremony and to the marriage of the couple.

Each of their children's christenings, which were performed in their first year, had similar creative elements. They made a medicine bag for each child and asked all the guests to bring a small token that symbolized a quality or protection that they wished to give the child. During the ceremony, each person came forward and placed their gift in the medicine bag with a blessing. As their children grow up and go through various changes, the parents take out the medicine bag and pull out one of the tokens that represents a quality or protection that can help them in that moment. These children have deeply appreciated the symbols of love and caring that offer them solace and empowerment in times of transition or challenge. I am honored to have participated in such conscientious and powerful ceremonies.

The most powerful ceremony I have ever attended was the memorial service for the wife of the president of the corporation for which I used to work. He had retired to be with his wife near the end of her long battle with cancer. The ceremony was held in Ojai, California, a place known for its spiritual power. It was sacred land for the Chumash in earlier days and is host to many diverse spiritual organizations today.

The ceremony was performed honoring feminine energy with earth-based ritual. Everyone who attended was invited to bring along drums. Many of the attendees were from the company and had not had prior experience with nature-based ceremony. At one point in the ceremony, we were invited to chant or sing the word MA, a sacred tone honoring feminine deity. The chanting led to drumming. A strong presence of spirit filled the natural setting.

People were also asked to bring cards with their thoughts and feelings written on them. They were tied to the leaves of a giant willow. It was a windy day and each time someone would come up to tell a story, the wind seemed to kick up at exactly the most emotional points, blowing the cards wildly about, sometimes into the body of the speaker. This may sound kind of phenomenal, but it is amazing how attuned nature is with ceremony.

When I have participated in outdoor ceremonies, it is common for a hawk to fly by right at a moment of significant power. Or in a sweat lodge, just as a solemn prayer is being spoken a rock will crackle or pop indicating that spirit agrees with the testimony.

Ceremony is like a turbocharged version of affirmation or visualization. It brings in physical energy and, in doing so, completes the manifestation process of thought, feeling, and action. The following ceremony is a powerful ritual that can be done to create newness in one's life. Each time I have performed it, many changes have occurred almost instantaneously. I only recommend practicing this if you are ready for change, because it can have powerful effects. The point of the ceremony is to release things (including behaviors, possessions, and even people) you no longer need in your life and bring things to you for which you are ready.

When I was still growing *Meditation* magazine, I performed this ceremony, and some of the most important staff members left the magazine the next week, people who were resisting the changing direction of the magazine. Within another week, there was an influx of new people who wanted to volunteer. It was clear afterward that the people who left were no longer meant to be involved in the project and the new people who came had exactly the energy and interest that was needed for future growth. So be specific in what you ask for; like the old saying goes, you might just get it.

This ritual can be done alone or with many people. Feel free to adapt it to fit your particular needs. It is excellent for starting a new project or career, ending or beginning a relationship, or clearing out psychological patterns that are no longer useful and is ideal as a new year's ceremony.

※　※　※

Ceremony for Release and Rebirth

Go to a special place in nature and bring with you a trowel or shovel, matches and writing paper, and a musical instrument or a drum, if you wish. Begin by singing a sacred song or chant, saying a prayer that has deep meaning to you, or simply drumming or playing an instrument— whatever will put you in a sacred space and in contact with the nature around you.

Meditate on the things you have in your life that you are thankful for including personal talents, relationships, opportunities, freedoms, possessions, and so on. Write them down on a piece of paper. Burn the paper in a way that keeps the nature around you safe. Sing or chant a meaningful song as you perform this task. Dig a small hole and bury the ashes. You can chant, sing, or play a musical instrument after this round and each subsequent round.

Meditate or pray about the things that you are ready to release in your life. It could be people, things, emotional patterns, attachments, fears, doubts, and so on. Write down all that comes to your mind that you would like to release. Repeat the burning and burying ritual while you again sing or chant. The things you have released have been transformed by the fire spirit, and as you plant the ashes in the earth, like seeds they will symbolically grow into something new and beautiful.

Meditate or pray about the things you want to bring into your life such as the kinds of people, projects, career, support, strengths, qualities, and so on. When you have finished, write them down and repeat the burning and burying ritual while singing or chanting. This time, the fire is purifying your prayers, and the earth will nurture them when they are buried.

Meditate or pray on how you will use your new gifts. Pray for others and how you can assist their growth. When you have finished, once again write them down and burn and bury them while singing or chanting.

Conclude by singing, drumming, chanting, laughing, dancing, praying, hugging (if you are in a group), or all of the above.

When you have finished, you may write down your goals so that you remember them, but this is not essential, for you will know them when they come into your life.

9

Magic in the Dark

Magic can work in times of illness, tragedy, even death, although it may not *feel* magical. When we are in despair, depressed, in pain, or ill, it is sometimes difficult, if not impossible, to expect a miracle. It is important to allow ourselves to go through the emotions naturally. Healing in itself is magic, and one way it occurs is by supporting ourselves through crisis and by striving to accept whatever situation is causing the crisis.

Give yourself love when you are hurt, when you have lost a love, when you have difficulties in your career, when you are sick. Be gentle with yourself. Cater to yourself. Hug yourself often and ask others for hugs. When you cannot see a silver lining in the dark clouds surrounding you, allow yourself to go into the darkness. Don't resist it. Look for the magic in the darkness. Affirm that a light still protects you in your dark place. Surrender to a power greater than you that can see the light. View your problems from the perspective of the source in addition to honoring the dark place from which your healing will arise.

No matter how great our pain is or how dark our path becomes from clouds blocking the sun's rays, the sun never leaves. The sun is still sending its nurturing, life-giving sustenance. As a symbol of our soul, it sees us through the clouds. It is with us every moment.

*Be in the dark, but know
that the sun is still there.*

We don't need darkness to appreciate the light, but inherent in the darkness is the longing to reach for the light. Our pain and suffering are liberators when we accept them as part of our path. Let them lead you to greater self-awareness, deeper self-understanding, and a purer expression of the magic of your soul.

The magic inherent in our sorrow and loss is illustrated by this passage by Gibran in *The Prophet.*

> The deeper that sorrow carves into your being, the more joy you can contain.
>
> Is not the cup that holds your wine, the very cup that was burned in the potter's oven?
>
> And is not the lute that fills your spirit, the very lute that was hollowed with knives?
>
> When you are joyous, look deep in your heart and you shall find that it is only that which has given you sorrow that is giving you joy.
>
> When you are sorrowful look again in your heart, and you shall see that in truth that you are weeping for your delight.[1]

HEALING

In our modern culture, people are accumulating many modern diseases that traditional medicine has not found effective means for treating. In fact, many of them are the result of or at least exacerbated by ineffective medical treatment, including the overprescription of antibiotics and other drugs, which lower the immune system and destroy the body's natural healing balance. Most of these modern diseases are in some way related to stress. Some of the common maladies are chronic stress syndrome, Epstein-Barr, fibromialgia, gastro-intestinal disorders, candida, antibiotic-resistant bacteria, persistent viral infection, etc.

If you find yourself with an ailment that is not improving with traditional treatment, find a reputable nutritionist and try alternative methods (not too many at a time), including hyperbaric oxygen, colon therapy, acupuncture and dry cupping, meditation, biofeedback, self-hypnosis, prayer, etc.

Become an expert on your condition. Healing sometimes requires the willingness to do whatever it will take to get well. Ask your angels or spiritual guides to find the right practitioners to help you heal. But do not turn over your power to the experts. With each remedy offered, check it with your own intuition. Research it carefully and understand any possible side effects. And finally test it with your experience. Continue to use the remedies that prove successful by improving your condition and eliminate those that do not pass your testing.

The best healer is your own mind. Develop a positive attitude. Know that you can and will heal yourself. Exercise as much as you can without exacerbating symptoms. If you cannot exercise, at least stretch every day. Meditate twice a day for at least twenty minutes. Achieving alpha brain waves in meditation or self-hypnosis can greatly reduce stress and condition the mind as a healing agent. You will know it is working if you develop a state of bliss on a regular basis. This may take weeks or months of practice, but if you can achieve this state on a regular basis, you will be employing the most powerful natural healing agent available—your own body chemistry. A blissful mind creates a natural chemical emission of endorphins, which puts your body in a state receptive to healing and supports any other strategy you employ.

In order to achieve a state of bliss, we must give up any fear we have about our condition. This may require surrendering to a higher power. It may require repeated surrendering to a higher power. I have found that the most effective attitude for healing is: 1) a positive attitude that affirms healing is imminent but also accepts the condition completely in the moment, and 2) an intense intent to do what is necessary to bring about the most complete healing possible combined with a surrendering to a higher power to guide the process.

But healing doesn't necessarily have to mean a perfectly healthy body. Perhaps disability is a healing for the psyche of someone needing to understand a deeper level of self than the body. Perhaps death is a healing, so we can move on to higher levels of expression once we have learned what we need from a particular life. Whatever our physical state, we can accept our limitations and learn who we are at a deeper level.

We *are* more than our bodies, and no matter how disabled the body becomes, we can still be bearers of light for the world. Affirming and practicing loving kindness while we have intense challenges is the most honorable and powerful expression of the magic of the soul. If we practice being a positive force when things are going well in our lives, we become a powerful human. If we can practice being a positive force when our very existence is being challenged, we become a force that supersedes our humanity. We move into the realm of the great spiritual models found throughout history.

Receive the light, become immersed
in it, be its emissary.

The beneficial function of illness is that we can learn from the symptoms of our limitations. Allow the symptoms to be your teachers. The symptoms of our disabilities often hold the key to healing. When I was very sick with chronic fatigue, my symptoms taught me to be at peace internally. They taught me how to use my energy in more efficient ways. They taught me to accept my limitations and remain a force of light regardless of the outer appearance of life. Learning and applying all of these lessons as well as the practical suggestions in this section is what led to my physical healing. Whatever your limitations at any moment in time, accept them and use them to propel you into a higher state of soul expression.

THE SOUL'S RESPONSE TO TRAGEDY

On September 11, 2001, three hijacked planes killed thousands as they slammed into the World Trade Center and the Pentagon. It was an act of terrorism and hatred designed to punish the enemies of extremists. The response to the violent act was varied and extreme.

In addition to the heroism of the rescue efforts and compassionate support in the form of donations for the victims' familiy, fear, anger, pain, desire for retribution, depression, even paralysis, were all responses witnessed and experienced by Americans and their friends around the world. Such is the case in other historical tragedies as well: the bombing of Pearl Harbor, the retaliatory nuclear attack on Japan, ethnic genocide by the Nazis and Serbs, and even the violent responses by America on Afghanistan and Iraq. In all of these cases, the victims of the violence had their lives shattered.

Such acts can be difficult to reconcile in the context of spiritual understanding. First, we must honor our humanness and embrace all the feelings such violent tragedy brings. This is prerequisite to healing, but it is also a necessary step in arriving at a higher understanding. When we venture into the depth of the pain in our hearts, and through it reach the love in our soul, we can see clearly the futility of violence and vengeance. We will be inspired to vow never to wish such pain or tragedy on any other human, and we will avoid actions, words, beliefs, and political policies that could contribute to violence both directly and indirectly.

The soul and the realm of spirit do not view tragedy as negative. This may seem impossible to understand, but the recognition at the soul level is that every, yes every, experience leads to growth and evolution. We don't always have the capacity to see a large enough picture to understand the purpose of the tragedies listed above, but the soul does.

If such violent tragedy has the capacity to exist, it must continue to manifest so that the evolution can occur that will preclude the possibility for such violent tragedy to exist. But with each experience of tragedy, we must choose the path that leads to the necessary evolution. If we don't, similar tragedies will continue to occur until the appropriate choice is made. This is true both on an individual level and on a national or international level.

September 11 was called a wake-up call. Wake-up call to what? To fear and greater self-protection? Clearly that was one result and perhaps rightfully and wisely so. It was also a wake-up call for the

United States to come together as a nation. It was a wake-up call to a deeper value system. The Wall Street idols that were built on material success in the 90s were replaced by firemen and social service people dedicated to helping others. It was also a wake-up call for many to the realization that such hatred still exists in the world. This is a truth realized by many people outside the United States who live in poverty, oppression, and fear every day of their lives. In times of tragedy, we can wake up to the spiritual and personal epiphany as a nation, group, or individual that is inherent in the tragedy. It could have been a wake-up call to come together as a world not only to wage war on terrorism but on war and violence of any kind. To recognize that every life is as valuable as every other life and to kill innocent people in the name of retribution or even justice is contradictory and certainly not an expression of soul.

An attitude of peaceful purpose was certainly a far cry from the sentiment of the general public in the wake of the disasters. Justice and even revenge were the popular outcry. In exploring ethical issues, I like to bring scenarios down to a personal level to look at them. If someone, God forbid, were to break into my house and kill my family, what might be my reaction? My first thought might be to find and kill the perpetrator. As difficult as it might be, however, I hope that my actions would be influenced by a deeper level of wisdom and compassion. I would want to do what I could to make certain that the individual would not commit the same crime against others, but without question, I would not kill innocent people to find the perpetrator. Neither would I vie for the death of the perpetrator. Ending any life is not consistent with divine intention. Although solving international terrorism is not as simple as this example, it is important to be mindful about the motivations of our actions. If we begin from a state of compassion, we will proceed with very different actions than if we begin from a state of vengeance.

To kill innocent people dishonors the lives and deaths of those who inspire the call to justice. Do the innocent victims of American bombs in Afghanistan deserve any less consideration than those who died in the September 11 attack? Any plan for justice that considers the killing of innocent people (collateral damage) as part of the equation is not a plan that truly seeks justice. Violence only breeds more violence. We must find solutions that protect and encourage life if we truly want to secure the world from terrorism. When we act from the magic of our souls and experience spiritual energy moving through us, we will always search for solutions that support life and growth.

I am not detached enough from my body to choose the path of Ghandi and face violence with passive resistance—to allow myself to be beaten as a way of demonstrating the futility of violence. I think I would choose to defend myself. But I must admit that Ghandi's way was a higher road that takes far more courage. Below is a true story about a man who displayed such courage.

Shortly after the coup that occurred in the former Soviet Union in 1990, a Russian psychologist named Igor Filippov stayed in my home for a few weeks. Only weeks before, he had been one of the Russian citizens who had created a barricade around their congressional house to protect it from attack by the Russian Military attempting to take power. The following is his description of the events surrounding the coup as it was printed in *Meditation* magazine.

> The beginning of the coup was like being in a movie. I was awakened at 6 a.m. by my friend's call, "Wake up! Turn on the TV and listen to the announcement of a new regime!" Listening to the TV, I couldn't stop thinking . . . not again!
>
> My American friend asked my opinion about the current situation. I answered that this will last either several days or several years. I was inclined to believe the latter. I vividly saw in my mind a picture of the Russian people passively going to their jobs in between the tanks and thinking: "That's life. There's nothing we can do about it." It was this kind of complacent attitude that has been common in Russia that the temporary regime was counting on.
>
> On the second day of the coup, we were informed that the attack would be that night. Many people went to defend the White House (nicknamed during the uprising). We created a human barricade to prevent the tanks from reaching the White House. The

prevailing feeling was one of peaceful resistance. You could hear cries of "No violence. Just stay and don't let them through. They won't dare crush a crowd of people."

Around 3 a.m., the tanks attacked the first row of the barricades. Many young adults jumped in front of the tanks. Two of them were crushed and another shot. The tanks stopped and the soldiers appeared at their tops. After some time, they turned the tanks around and left. They could not bring themselves to continue killing innocent people for their cause.[2]

The power of the soul triumphs. Many of our historical heroes are those who were fearless in battle. How much more inner strength and courage does it take to die in the name of peace than in the name of war? Had the Soviet citizens started a riot against the tanks, a bloody slaughter would have been the likely result. Their passive resistance ended the conflict with fewer but more heroic deaths. The only way we will ever end violence is to act with peaceful intention in all situations.

There are other stories of courage and compassion about individuals who have risen above fear, grief, and loss to embrace a higher principle. In 1993, Amy Biehl, a straight-A student from California, had gone to South Africa to help in the struggle against apartheid and to support women's rights in the country's first democratic elections. She was stoned to death by an angry mob who mistook her for a white South African. Her parents, Peter and Linda Biehl, launched a foundation the following year to carry on their daughter's commitment to human rights, democracy, and the aspirations of women and children in South Africa. In addition to going beyond their pain and loss to support a need that was associated with their daughter's death, they actually testified in support of amnesty for her murderers in the Truth and Reconciliation hearings that were held to bring healing to the community.

Another inspiring example is the story of Laura Bloomfield, which can be found in her book titled *Revenge*. In 1986, her father, a noted Rabbi, was shot by a member of the PLO. He eventually fully recovered from the attack, but Laura became obsessed with getting revenge for the incident. She traveled to Europe and the Middle East researching methods of revenge for terrorism. She went undercover to Palestine to meet the attacker's family. Through her direct contact with the constant pain and terror in the region, she developed a deeper understanding of the plight of the Palestinian people and her father's assailant. Eventually, she met the target of her anger in prison, learned that he was deeply sorry for his crime, and even spoke in his defense at his trial. Imagine the deepening of one's self-understanding to rise to such a height of forgiveness. I get chills every time I speak or write about this story. Nearly everyone would be inspired by such selfless action, yet often we are unable to forgive those who have committed far less critical grievances. Peace will prevail when people everywhere go deep into their hearts to find compassion, which is the only force that can heal our conflicts on both individual and global levels.

---

*Journey to the center of your heart
and embrace the love that can heal all conflict.*

Every event holds a spiritual lesson, even those that do not have perpetrators. Disasters—earthquakes, floods, death by natural causes, or accidents—all open our humanity to a higher spiritual understanding. If no other lesson is understood, there is the basic truth as taught in Buddhism that everything in physical form is impermanent. Every human loss is an affirmation and reminder that a truer reality exists beyond the level of form. The only way to peace in the face of physical loss is to accept spirit.

WHY DOES DEATH SEEM SO UNREAL?

Most people who experience the loss of a loved one are perplexed by the seeming impossibility that they could be here one moment—sharing experience, fully present—and the next moment (or day or week or month), they are no longer around. It is the seeming impossibility of the phenomenon of death that indicates the reality of its illusion. Death seems impossible because it is. Nothing ever dies; it only changes form. When someone passes, our senses experience death, but if we are in tune with the truth, we will experience the continuance of life in a new form.

Gibran also writes about death in *The Prophet*.

> Your fear of death is but the trembling of the shepherd when he stands before the king whose hand is to be laid upon him in honor.
>
> Is the shepherd not joyful beneath his trembling, that he shall wear the mark of the king?
>
> Yet is he not more mindful of his trembling?
>
> For what is it to die and stand naked melting into the sun?
>
> And what is it to cease breathing, but to free your breath from its restless tides, that it may rise and expand and seek God unencumbered?
>
> Only when you drink from the river of silence shall you indeed sing.
>
> And when you reach the mountain top, then you shall begin to climb.
>
> And when the earth shall claim your limbs, then shall you truly dance.[3]

This doesn't mean that we shouldn't grieve the loss of our sensory experience with someone we love who graduates to another level of existence. As souls with human bodies, we are both human and divine, and it is just as important to honor our humanness as it is to honor the truth of our divine nature. Give yourself permission to cry and scream and mourn as much and as long as you need. But also recognize the truth that you can never lose anyone. In fact, when the barrier of physical reality is dissolved, the opportunity for spiritual communion is even greater. While fully grieving the loss of the sensory relationship, seek to enhance your ongoing spiritual relationship. And continue to embrace and be in awe of the magic that exists in all experience.

Cry your pain.
Scream your rage.
Shudder with your fear.
You are strong enough to face anything.
You will endure.
You become stronger
as you embrace your weakness.

Allow!

Accept the peace when it comes.
Relish it.
Bathe in it.
Let it fill your heart.
Share it in all that you do.
Every experience in life is magical.

Below is a description from a close friend, Bob Lesoine (who is also the talented musician who created the background music for *The Magic of the Soul* CD), of the passing of his mother earlier this year. The way he cared for and released his mother was a touching, inspirational, and magical expression of soul.

Mom is eighty-eight and in the last stages of Alzheimer's, which means she has forgotten how to eat or swallow or speak. She has been withdrawing into her dementia, just tuning out, for quite a while now. We have chosen not to put her on an I.V. The doctor says it would just prolong the inevitable.

When I enter her room, Mom lies in bed, eyes wide open, staring unblinkingly at something beyond the ceiling. Her mouth is open in awe of . . . I don't know what. She gives no acknowledgment that I am there. She does not communicate. But the doctor tells me she probably does hear everything. Then I kiss her forehead and tell her that I love her. I thank her for her love, for being my mother, for giving me birth, and for giving me the greatest gift—music!

The next day I return to the hospital. How do you learn to wait with your mother for her death? It isn't easy. Mom continues to lay, mouth open in the "O" of a silent moan. Today, her open mouth seems more like a shout or a scream of terror. She seems in distress as if during the night she'd been wrestling with her demons. It's disturbing to see her like this.

I take her withered, skeletal hand from beneath the covers and hold it. I begin the Buddhist om-ah-hung purification chant. When I get tired, I perform Tonglin exchange breath meditation in the periods of silence. I take in all her fear and confusion on my in-breath and breathe out loving kindness and compassion for her. It's like a compassion pump. In and out. In and out. Then I read to her from the book written by my Buddhist teacher Lama Khenpo Konchog Gyaltshen Rinpoche, *The Transformation of Suffering: A Handbook for Practitioners.*

When I return to her room later that evening, I read more to her and explain that in his teachings, the Buddha asks us to understand the illusory nature of all existence by meditating on such things as magic shows, dreams, echoes, reflections, dew, bubbles, mirages, and rainbows. I explain to her that these are things we experience as real manifestations, but they are merely illusions. The teaching is trying to help us understand that our bodies, our experiences, our lives as they unfold—the very "I" that we cling to as solid and permanent—all of these can also be seen as similar illusions. Once we see them as such, we can stop being attached to them and let them go. I urge Mom to let go of this old, shriveled, skeletal body. "It's OK to just let go now," I tell her. "You can leave this existence, though I will miss you. It will be all right." We end the evening by meditating together with her hand in mine.

The next day when I return to the hospital her breath is coming in short gasps. She makes a slightly audible "ah, ah, ah" sound with each out-breath. I greet her and whisper in her ear, "Bob's here. It's me, your son, Bob, who loves you." I caress her forehead and neck. I pull the retracted claw of her hand from beneath her covers. It is warm to the touch today.

As I hold her hand, I begin to thank her again for everything I can think of, for all she's been to me as a mother and friend. "Mom, thank you for giving birth to me. Thank you for your smile. Thank you for your laughter. Thank you for all the meals you've cooked for me. Thank you for the flowers you've grown, for the beautiful orchids you raised. Thank you for making my bed and sleeping in my room when I was a child and I was afraid in the night." The thanks are endless. There will never be enough time to say them all.

I notice that she has been doing the ahs with each breath for the past couple of days. Buddhists believe that the "ah" purifies all negative karma generated through speech. I realize that Mom, who sometimes had a sharp, judgmental tongue, has been unconsciously purifying her speech for the past few days. ah . . . ah . . . ah. Perhaps this is why she's been waiting. So again I take up the OM-ah-hung mantra, but now I time it so Mom's ah comes in between my OM and hung. Pretty soon, we've coordinated the rhythm and are in sync purifying body (om), speech (ah), and mind (hung) over and over.

My friend Corlene, who knew my mother many years before, asked if she could come and pay her last respects. Corlene had experience as a hospice worker. She joins us in the chanting. I can't say exactly how long we continue this. After an indeterminate period of silence, I begin to slowly sing the melodic om-mani-padme-hung chant that Khenpo taught me when I took the Chenrezig empowerment seminar. This is done to cultivate loving kindness and compassion for all sentient beings who have been our mothers throughout infinite space and time. I am surprised that Corlene joins right in and sings it flawlessly with me as if she had known it all her life.

We chant on, "om-mane-padme-hung" over and over and

over, and then finally I end it with a "hri!" We sit in silence for I don't know how long. Then, I notice it is really silent. More silent than it had ever been. At that point, I open my eyes and look at Mom. Her mouth is still wide open. Her eyes still open looking upward but no longer seeing. There is no movement in her chest or throat. I listen for her "ah" breaths. Nothing. I looked at Corlene. "This could be it." I say. "I think so." She agrees.

My first impulse is to let the nurse check and listen for a heart-beat. But Corlene says, "Just take this time for you and her alone." I just sit with Mom for a while longer.

Finally, I put my ear close to her still-open mouth to check for breath. What I hear is the roar of the ocean as if lifting a seashell to my ear but no breath. It is over. She passes at 1:05 p.m.

Strangely now, a day later as I write this, I do not feel sadness. I feel elation. I feel uplifted by being able to experience Mom's death. Immediately afterward, I felt like running down the halls of the nursing home shouting, "Death is *not* the enemy!" Maybe the fear of death but certainly not death itself. Mom's was so natural. I almost wrote *easy* but it was not easy. But natural, yes. A completion, yes. Right, yes. In the past day or so, when a friend or relative has said to me that they are sorry or, "It's all so sad," I say, "No, it's not sad." When we learn that a prisoner has been released from prison, are we sad? Mom is free now. The songbird has taken flight.

Bob did mourn the loss of his mother in the days and weeks following her death. He cried in my presence. His sadness was testimony to his deep love for his mother. But his affirmation, his absolute belief that her spirit, her soul, was still alive and that he can still celebrate her ongoing life is his highest testimony of love.

As with every experience in life, we can let death, sickness, or loss control us by reacting to it, or we can accept it, experience it in the depth of our being, and treat it as a magical moment in time—a moment that will never be available again. Each moment contains an opportunity to experience life in a different way, a deeper way. Get the most out of every experience that you can.

In my moments of deepest depression and frustration when I was extremely sick and mourning the loss of love, I felt lost. My magic seemed to fail me. But I continued to believe there was a way out even though I couldn't see it. Although I had no idea of how to heal and get my life back, I held on to hope. I communicated with my angels and affirmed that even in my dark place, there was light surrounding me. I sometimes resisted my situation, but each resistance led to a greater level of surrender and acceptance. The acceptance led to peace and a more profound understanding of myself as spirit—a recognition that at a spiritual level, nothing could hurt me—everything I was experiencing would lead me to a higher expression of my soul.

The exercise below, created by Dr. Vivian King can be done when you are in times of despair, challenge, or life transition. Give yourself the light of your highest self when you are in need.

☀   ☀   ☀

Sun Meditation
(Track 11 on Audio CD)

Imagine you are standing on the highest mountaintop and gazing out at the world in all directions. To the east is the rising sun. You feel its loving warmth on your skin. Drink in the sunshine with your pores and pay homage to the sun spirit with your mind and soul. Be aware of a single golden ray streaming forth from the sun and enveloping you. Feel the sunlight transforming your body as it bathes you outside and within. Your body becomes lighter as though it is becoming the light of the ray itself. Your molecular structure changes as you become sunlight. Your awareness is now traveling through the sunbeam toward the sun. As you approach the heavenly orb, the light becomes more intense and the life-giving energy more pure. You are not afraid because you are of the same nature as the sun. As you enter the sun's atmosphere, your consciousness explodes and becomes one with the sun. What does it feel like to be the sun, radiating love and life in all directions? Feel the power as your awareness envelops all that the light from the sun reaches. Feel how enormous is your span of consciousness.

Now be aware of your personality back on earth. As the sun, a symbol of your soul, observe your personality in its daily activities. What do you see from this high perspective? What message would you like to communicate to your earthly self? Communicate it through your light. As the sun, how do you feel when your personality has blocked your light with clouds of doubt or fear? What is your message to yourself in these times? Communicate that message with your light. What else would you like to send to your persona?

Allow your awareness to focus on your personality and be aware of that one golden stream of light that connects you to your body. Allow your awareness to travel through the beam, bringing the nurturing love of the sun, of your soul, through the stream to your personality. Say your name over and over as you approach your body. Bring the love and perspective into your body and feel it in your heart. Breathe deeply as you fully accept the love and support of your soul consciousness.

Follow your Bliss
Do what we love to do

What's light your to shine?

"*The purpose of life is to find your talent & give it away*"

10

Purpose

Once we have provided for our basic needs in life—food, safety, security, and love—the largest question that we face is the meaning of life. Why are we here? In general, it is to be part of that Creative Principle working through all life. But what is our individual and specific purpose? Each individual has a unique role through which they support the evolution of the planet and of the human species. The expression of purpose through one's life is possibly the highest aspect of the magic of the soul. Life purpose and soul purpose are synonymous. When we embrace and empower our purpose through our careers, through all of our activities in life, a wide channel opens from the heart of the soul allowing its magic to flow into our lives and all those we touch.

What is your purpose in life?

I don't necessarily mean what you do for a living, although there is a relationship between the two. What do you like to do that contributes in some way to making the world a better place? Do you like to teach, make people smile, make people laugh, create, create beautiful things, crunch numbers, play games, solve problems, empower others, organize, discover principles, inspire, contribute to health, release trapped emotion, awaken spiritual awareness? Whatever the answer:

This is your purpose!

If your job does not answer the question above, then it is not directly fulfilling your purpose. But every purpose has the potential to be fulfilled to some degree through every possible career. It may require a shifting of intent to infuse soul purpose into a career that may not appear to contribute to making the world a better place. By recognizing and committing to soul purpose, we can apply it anywhere and everywhere. We must begin by clarifying our soul purpose.

Another way to help define your purpose is to contemplate your vision of an ideal world. How would you describe a perfect world?

A world where people are supportive of one another?

A world filled with beauty?

A world filled with order and justice?

A world where children feel safe and nurtured?

A world where adults can still play?

A world of peace?

Write down your answer and how can you contribute to creating that vision. The goal is not necessarily to achieve an ideal world but to use the vision to move us toward the ideal. The magic is in the process, not the result.

Now write down what was missing in your childhood. What did you not receive from your parents that you are still developing for yourself? I have found in countless workshops that there is a direct correlation between what we did not receive as children and our ideal world.

For example, if you were not nurtured, you may envision a world where everyone is nurtured or where children in particular are nurtured. You may find that nurturing others gives you the greatest feeling of satisfaction. You could find that whatever your job, it is most fulfilling for you when you are able to nurture others. In this example, to find your ideal career, you could set a plan, get the necessary education and training, and become a health practitioner so that you are paid a good salary for nurturing others to optimal health.

The powerful message in this understanding is that what we are healing for ourselves is our gift to the world. The great author and poet, Robert Bly says that "our wound is our gift." We don't have to get to a place where we are healed in order to succeed at fulfilling our purpose successfully. In fact, it is our struggle to provide for ourselves what we didn't receive as a child that develops within us the tools to teach it to others, to contribute to the ideal world. We fulfill our service best when we take our wound with us, when we share it openly in our service, for this is what will most inspire those we will teach and serve. *(self-esteem / empowerment)*

We come into this life choosing our challenges, imperfections, potential, and all the experiences that make us who we are. As souls, we choose our challenges and limitations so we can evolve as souls through developing them. We are inspired to develop the qualities that we lack and, ultimately, to help others develop them as well, either directly or indirectly through our purpose.

Write down on a piece of paper the answers to all of the following questions: How many different careers could you fulfill through your purpose? How do you fulfill it now? How could you fulfill it more fully in your current situation? What career would most directly and effectively fulfill your purpose? Write down the steps you could take if you decided to fulfill your purpose through your ideal career.

Many people feel they are trapped in jobs that are not fulfilling because they have to make a living. They can't make as much money doing what they want to do—that which would contribute more fully to the well-being of others, to making the world a better place.

My experience has proven to me that such a belief system (I held it at one time, and at times it still holds me) is erroneous. It is directly in contrast to the way of the magic of the soul. Much of it stems from the long-entrenched social viewpoint that life is a struggle.

As you begin to implement your plan to create the most direct fulfillment of your purpose through career, look for opportunities to fulfill it in every interaction you have with others. Ask others for help. Offer to help those whom you can. Acknowledge everyone who gives you assistance (as publicly as possible). The most powerful tool to success, besides your own unique soul power, is your interactions that empower others to manifest their life purpose.

A JOURNEY OF PURPOSE

I began my adult career as a tennis pro, empowering people to see a deeper connection to life through physical exercise, visualization techniques, and Zen tennis. At the time, I believed I would never do anything other than teach tennis, as it was so fulfilling to me. But as I succeeded in fulfilling my purpose through teaching tennis, I became inspired to teach spiritual principles on a deeper level, so I decided to become a minister. In 1985, I was teaching a class called the Nature of the Soul, written by Lucile Cedercrans. Much of the information was centered around soul magic and the expression of purpose in service to the world and humanity. Every time I started this particular teaching, something was created, and this time the idea that emerged was to create a magazine called *Meditation*. The original staff was made up of the six individuals who were taking the class. It began as a volunteer project and everyone working on it had other jobs to support themselves. No one had any experience in the publishing industry, but we committed to creating a successful and valuable product that would contribute to a better world. The project was not an overnight success. Although it did in time support modest salaries for the core staff, it never rose to the level of financial viability for which I had hoped and meditated, but I have always considered it a profoundly meaningful and successful endeavor.

I had left a successful career as a tennis professional to do what I believed was more meaningful work. I went out on a limb, so to speak, and was blessed for the risk. The skills I learned during my time as executive editor, advertising director, writer, typesetter, distribution manager, and paste-up artist were all part of what led me to success in future publishing incarnations and also gave me a great start on how to write and publish this book.

When we stopped publishing the magazine, I had to decide what I would do next for income. My greatest joy was writing and teaching, but I didn't want to do the job of promoting myself as a teacher. I knew I could make good money in sales or management, but I was not interested in selling and I was pretty burned out on responsibility, so management was unappealing. I wanted to work on my writing, but also needed an income. I didn't want to write as a job, because I would be doing that in my spare time. The job function of the magazine that I enjoyed most on a day-to-day basis was typesetting, which I did for about three weeks once every three months. So I decided to apply for typesetting positions. I became excited about the prospect of doing some creative work that would require little left-brain activity and would allow me lots of reserve to be creative in my writing projects.

I was turned down for two jobs and then found an opening at Sage Publications, an academic publisher that was using the same outdated version of Ventura Publisher (a desktop publishing software) that I had used at the magazine—a perfect fit. I began making a modest salary. Within a year, I was promoted to supervisor and six months later to managing editor. In another three years, I made it to director and was working my way toward VP. During my time at Sage, I learned how to apply my spiritual ideals in a corporate setting and was known for my leadership abilities in empowering employees in their jobs, which also bled into other areas of their lives. The experience I received by implementing spiritual principles in such a contrasting arena as corporate management increased my understanding of the magic of the soul. My success affirmed that the practice worked. I was the last person others would have expected to excel in a corporate environment, given my metaphysical leaning. Not only did I succeed at dramatically improving systems within the company, I also taught the magic of the soul indirectly through my management style and directly through my daily stress-reduction meetings that I offered to anyone in the company who wished to participate. The next book I write will most likely be on integrating spiritual principles through corporate management.

As a result of my illness and the wisdom I gained from it, I no longer had the desire to be part of the frantic and competitive corporate world. I had started at Sage to earn a living to support my writing career, and my strategy was to go back into the teaching arena, once I had written and published a book that would draw people to the teaching. I had already written one book, a novel called *The Dark Night of the Soul,* a metaphysical horror story of transformation, and was working on this book when I became ill. My illness is what led to my departure from Sage and also to an understanding that allowed me to complete this book with a depth that I had not intended when I began writing it. Had I continued moving up the corporate ladder at lightning speed, I might not have ever completed this book, much less written as valuable a piece as I believe it has become. Valuable at least for me, and I hope it is valuable to you as well.

To sum up my path of purpose: My desire to help others on a deeper level, which was born out of my career in teaching tennis, led me to empower larger numbers of people through writing articles and publishing *Meditation* magazine while teaching workshops to empower people on a more personal basis. At the end of it, I again followed my heart by taking the job that gave me the most delight, which led me to empowering people and applying spiritual principles in perhaps one of the most difficult places to apply them—a corporate culture. That path led me to the writing of this book and a renewed desire to empower through teaching—this system called "the magic of the soul."

The important lessons in this journey were 1) that I made choices that were based on what I really wanted to do regardless of how difficult it may have seemed to succeed, and 2) that I was fulfilling my purpose in each career, which always led to a higher expression of my purpose. There were many times that I had doubts about where my path was leading me. There were struggles to balance my spiritual service with financial responsibilities. But through it all, I always trusted (or at the very least, tested the hypothesis) that what I enjoyed doing and what contributed to the lives of others would lead me along the most magical path.

Try acting on the hypothesis that
what makes you happy and fulfilled at a
soul level is what will bring you the most success.

SERVICE—FULFILLING A NEED

Most truly creative and successful people reject the belief that life is a struggle. They take the necessary steps to develop their talent in a way that creates a demand—they fulfill a need. This is an important point. In pop psychology and some new age systems of thought, the phrase "follow your bliss" has had a strong influence. But to be truly successful, it is imperative that we not only do that which is fulfilling to ourselves, but also that which is fulfilling to others. The basic premise of economy is service. In earlier days, our economy worked on the barter system. I would give you something that you needed in exchange for what I needed. Money was a convenient way of extending the bartering process. But the use of money has minimized the service aspect of economy. It has created a potential for exchange that results in far more surplus than any person can possibly need. This has created disturbances in our economic system that has caused a great gap between the few rich and the many poor.

But at the heart of economy is still the premise of service. We will supersede the limitations of our economic system any time we offer our purpose in a way that fulfills a need in society. In today's society, fulfilling a need also necessitates marketing. Not only do we have to fulfill the need, but we have to offer it in a way that the marketplace becomes aware of its availability and usefulness.

Make a list of your talents, skills, and all the things that you love to do that can contribute to a better world. Brainstorm with a friend or friends to see how you could utilize the elements on your list to create a wildly successful career that expresses your magical soul purpose. Once you have clarity about your ideal career, write a business plan that includes the need you are fulfilling, who your market is, and how you will reach it. Include all of the steps you will take and the skills you must develop to be successful. Also include dates of implementing plans for growth. Realize that your plan will change as your career grows, but it is immensely helpful to have a map to begin your journey.

That which fulfills our greatest purpose is our greatest achievement. Trying to fulfill that purpose challenges us to face our strongest blocks and, if successful, will uncover our greatest demons. It will also bring us the greatest joy and the most magic we can possibly imagine. Once you are clear on your purpose, pay close attention to the voices that come up telling you that you cannot achieve such a delicious expression of yourself. Do the exercises in this book that help you believe in your own magic and . . .

Fly sister fly!
Fly brother fly!

When you fully realize what your purpose is, begin to fulfill it as much as possible in your current vocation. Some people think that they cannot fulfill their purpose until they switch occupations. If your purpose is to teach love and your occupation is to make bombs, it will be difficult to reconcile your purpose with your career. Begin by teaching love in every way possible while making bombs. Share love with the people with whom you make bombs. Inspire a vision of a world where bombs are not necessary. It is much more effective to fulfill your purpose where you are rather than trying to get to a place in the future where you can begin to fulfill your purpose. As you teach love more effectively while making bombs, the path to your ideal career will automatically become more clear. As you become more proficient at fulfilling your purpose, doors open magically, allowing you to increasingly fulfill it with greater influence, results, and rewards.

Find Happiness + Joy where you are right now!!

Fulfill your purpose however you can, wherever you are. Surrender to a higher will—"Thy will be done" rather than my will. If you have a vision for how you can best fulfill your soul purpose and it hasn't worked out yet, accept that it means you need to become more proficient at fulfilling your purpose exactly where you are. Focus on increasing your effectiveness in fulfilling your purpose right now. Remind yourself consistently that you are here to serve. In this way you connect to the power of the Creative Principle, which then flows through everything you do.

As you increase your ability to fulfill your purpose, your personality will change. You will receive more light and radiate more light through the activities of your service. More effective means of fulfilling your purpose will become clear. Obstacles to fulfilling your purpose will fade as you recognize the truth: It doesn't matter *how* you fulfill your purpose but only that you fulfill it. One way to look at it is that if the universe gives you no better opportunity to serve than the situation you find yourself in presently, then you don't have to do anything else. Leave it up to the universe. Strive effortlessly— in a way that inspires you to give more—and accept that you need not do anything more than express your purpose wherever you are in each moment to the best of your ability.

Combine surrender with your practical steps and let the integration become the magical elixir that guides you along your path of discovery. Visualize yourself successfully fulfilling your purpose in all that you do. Be aware of the quality of energy you radiate through all your actions. One thing is certain, if you have a pure intention to be of service, you will succeed, and your expression of service will continually become more beneficial to others and more fulfilling to you.

The following exercise is adapted from a meditation printed in *Meditation* magazine as part of an article on Sandy Levey-Lunden and her *Art of Personal Marketing*.[1] Sandy Levey-Lunden is a dynamic spiritual teacher who profoundly influenced my understanding and application of purpose in my life through her one-weekend seminar.

☀ ☀ ☀

Exercise on Purpose

For free audio version, http://www.livingpurposeinstitute.com/meditation.htm

This is best done with a partner but can be done alone using the audio version at the link above. Sit facing each other and decide who will ask the question first and who will answer. One asks, "If you could do anything you want in relation to fulfilling your purpose through career, what would it be?" The partner replies with the first thing that comes to mind. The asker repeats the question. Continue with the process for at least fifteen repetitions. The point is to go beyond the first few obvious answers and get to areas that have previously been unexplored by the conscious mind. The asker can facilitate the creative process by asking the question with different phrasings and inflections: For example: If you had no limitations, what would you do to fulfill your purpose? If you had complete and total freedom, how would you make your purpose felt in the world?

☀ ☀ ☀

When our soul purpose becomes aligned with and fully active in our daily activities, we become filled with a profound inner peace. We become the soul working through the aligned personality. We gain access to spiritual magic that will assist us in achieving higher and higher expressions of our soul intent. We become the magic of our souls radiating outward to bring light to all that we can influence.

Be your soul purpose.

For an interactive tool to create a life purpose definition in less than ten minutes, please visit http://www.livingpurposeinstitute.com.

11

You Are the Magic

This book, others like it, and all of the many teachers and methods of inspiring transformation call us to become more, to claim and express a higher level of our potential. As I have said many times in different ways throughout this book, we are all on a path of discovery, and at the same time, we don't need to go anywhere. It is all right here, where we are in the moment. If you never grew or evolved any more than you have up to this point in your life (which would be impossible, of course), you would be perfect just the way you are. All the growth you experience beyond this point is icing on the cake, the blossoming of an already perfectly beautiful rose.

The exercise below is similar to the Magician of the Soul exercise in chapter 3. It can also be used as a self-assessment. Now that you have nearly completed the book, you may find it interesting to note any differences in self-assessment between now and when you did the Magician of the Soul exercise. This exercise also represents a way of empowering yourself through recognizing your own beauty. I highly recommend the book *Being Here When I Need Me*, by the late Dr. Vivian King, which contains her version of this exercise.[1]

❋   ❋   ❋

The Rose
(Track 12 on Audio CD)

Imagine that you are looking at a rosebush that represents your life as it is now. Observe the overall qualities of the rosebush. What do the flowers look like? What color are they? Smell their fragrance. Is it sweet? Are they full and open, or are they closed? Are they old and withered or are they fresh and healthy? What about the leaves on the bush? Are they a bright, healthy green or are they brown and dry? What about the stems and branches? Are they strong? Are they too thin and easily whisked about by the wind? Are they too rigid and therefore inflexible? Are there enough thorns for self-protection? Are there more thorns than necessary? Does your rosebush need pruning? Has it been well cared for?

What about the trunk of the bush? Is it strong enough? Is it healthy and does it aptly support the rest of the bush? Are the roots deep and wide or are they shallow and narrow? Is the soil rich in nutrients or is it in need of nourishment? Is the soil moist enough? Is there too much water, creating a muddy, unstable base?

What is the quality of the environment surrounding your rosebush? Is there enough light? What is the proximity of your rosebush to others? Are there other rosebushes nearby, or is it alone? Are there other bushes or plants growing into your rosebush? Is the sun shining or is the sky cloudy? Step back from your rosebush and assess what it needs most. Open your eyes and write what you have observed.

Close your eyes again and imagine that you are an expert gardener who represents your caring, loving self. Again assess what your rosebush needs. Now take as much time as you need to care for and improve the condition of your rosebush. In your imagination all things are possible, so you can do years of work in just minutes or seconds. Any tools you need are available to you. If you need assistance, you can call in other experts in irrigation or transplanting if it is necessary. When you have completed the work, open your eyes and write down a description of your gardening or share with a partner.

Close your eyes again and view your rosebush from the perspective of your loving gardener in the future, after enough time has lapsed for all your nurturing work to have taken effect. Feel the sense of pride welling up in your heart as you appreciate the beauty of your rosebush—of you. . . . Now allow your awareness to become your rosebush. Feel your roots stretching deep into the earth, drawing in nutrients from the soil. Feel your petals stretching to the sky, absorbing the warmth of the bright sunshine. See the smiling face of your gardener admiring your beauty with heartfelt pride. Allow yourself to indulge in the love and appreciation from your gardener. You deserve every bit of love being offered. You are beautiful. You are magical. You are the magic of the soul.

Much of the symbolism in this exercise is explained in the language or can be easily interpreted or intuited by the reader. Below are some general guidelines that may be helpful.

The roses and leaves can represent one's connection with the outside world.

The trunk can represent the basic foundation of the individual, the strength, or the will.

The roots can represent one's ancestry or one's depth and groundedness.

The soil can represent the quality of nurturing or health.

The moisture in the soil can represent emotional well-being. (Too much moisture could mean an abundance of emotion; dryness, a lack of emotion.)

The other rose bushes can represent relationships.

The sun or light can represent the soul.

The gardener generally represents the centered self—the part of you that cares for you.

This book as well as most discussions of the subject speak of the soul as something we possess. We speak about it this way out of convenience or convention. The truth is that we *are* the soul, and our expression in life is the reflection of our soul magic. I honor you as soul. There is no expression of consciousness in the entire universe that is exactly like you—like your expression of spirit in this world. No one else can contribute to the continuing evolution of all that is in the same way that you can. Your contribution is needed and essential just as everyone else's. I invite you to work with me in inspiring others to experience the magic that you have experienced through this book and the other significant spiritual realizations of your life. I thank you for your spirit, your interest in this topic, your diligence in learning and growing through your challenges, and your conscious participation in the magic of this wondrous journey we call life.

You are the Magic of the Soul!

Live your magic!

Author's Note

I am interested in your experiences as you practice *The Magic of the Soul*. Please visit my website at **www.livingpurposeinstitute.com** to give me feedback or to find out other ways of participating in this ongoing teaching. If you have questions about *The Magic of the Soul*, I would be happy to answer them online. In addition to the site, you can call me **toll free at (866) 204-2261** for information on the Life Purpose Coaching Certification Program, classes, teleseminars, workshops, Primal Fire Retreats, phone coaching, board retreats, speaking, or corporate trainings. I sometimes do take on new clients who have just finished the book and are really inspired. If I am not able to, we have certified life coaches to whom we can refer you. I would also love for you to augment your spiritual growth, and at the same time participate in a worldwide effort to **create Peace, Prosperity, and Perfect Health for all** by participating in The MAP: Manifesting Affirmation Process. For a free e-report on this revolutionary group support practice, visit www.affirmationmap.com. I would also be most grateful if you would consider doing a customer review of the book at amazon.com. Many thanks for reading, and I hope to meet you soon.

May your highest visions continue to be fulfilled!

Patrick J. Harbula

Additional Copies

For additional copies of *The Magic of the Soul*, please send $18.95 for each book (shipping is now free) to:

Peak Publications
2593 Young Avenue
Thousand Oaks, CA 91360
Or call toll free (866) 204-2261
or go to www.livingpurposeinstitute.com

Notes

Chapter 1: Spiritual Magic

1. Kahlil Gibran, *The Prophet*, p. 52.
2. Carlos Castaneda, *Journey to Ixlan*, p. 249.
3. Patrick Harbula, "Warrior Sage—Stuart Wilde," *Meditation*, winter 1990, p. 26.

Chapter 2: The Soul

1. Patrick Harbula, "Just Another Fairy Tail?" *Meditation*, fall 1990, p. 25.
2. Deepak Chopra, *How to Know God: The Soul's Journey Into the Mystery of Mysteries*, p. 203.

Chapter 3: Applying Magic

1. Kahlil Gibran, *The Prophet*, p. 21.
2. Willam Aldridge, "Man with No Arms," *Meditation*, fall 1986, pp. 24-25. Reprinted with permission from *Meditation* magazine.
3. Ken Keyes Jr., *The Hundredth Monkey*.
4. Rupert Sheldrake, *Meditation*, summer 1991, p. 22.

Chapter 4: God

1. Raynord C. Johnson, *The Imprisoned Splendor*.
2. Payne and Bendit, *The Psychic Sense*, pp. 183-84.
3. Richard Jefferies, *The Story of My Heart*, p. 199.
4. W. L. Wilmherst, *Contemplations*, p. 142.
5. Patrick Harbula, "Pir Vilayat Inayat Khan," *Meditation*, spring 1987, p. 16.
6. Patrick Harbula, "Many Roads Home," *Meditation*, summer 1988, p. 30.
7. Chief Seattle, "Our Sacred Earth," *Meditation*, spring 1989, pp. 34-35. Reprinted with permission from *Meditation* magazine.
8. Gary Zukav, *The Seat of the Soul*, p. 101.

Chapter 5: The Magic of Thought

1. W. T. Jones, ed., *The Classical Mind*, pp. 135-37.
2. Fritjof Capra, *The Tao of Physics*, p. 68.
3. Deana McInstry, "Quantum Healing: An Interview with Deepak Chopra," *Meditation*, fall 1992, p. 47.
4. Carlos Castaneda, *Tales of Power*, p. 252.
5. Foundation for Inner Peace, *A Course in Miracles*.

6. Ursula Niebuhr, ed., *Justice and Mercy: Reinhold Niebuhr.*

7. Ekhart Tolle, *The Power of Now*, p. 17.

Chapter 6: The Magic of Feeling

1. Violet S. deLaszlo, ed., *The Basic Writings of C. G. Jung*, p. 305.

2. Gary Zukav, *The Seat of the Soul*, p. 84.

3. Ekhart Tolle, *The Power of Now*, p. 69.

4. Roberto Assagioli, *Psychosynthesis*, p. 22.

Chapter 7: The Magic of Sensation.

1. Brooks Atkinson, "Nature," *The Selected Writings of Ralph Waldo Emerson*, pp. 406-7.

Chapter 8: Meditation

1. Mark Vancil, ed., *For the Love of the Game: My Story by Michael Jordan*, p. 64.

2. Arcane School, 120 Wall Street, 24th Floor, New York, NY 10005, www.arcaneschool.org/triangles/.

3. The World Peace Prayer Society, 26 Benton Road, Wassaic, NY 12592, (845) 877-6093, www.worldpeace.org, e-mail: info@worldpeace.org.

4. C. Borland & G. Landrith, "Improved Quality of City Life through the Transcendental Meditation Program: Decreased Crime Rate."

5. Carlos Castaneda, *Journey to Ixlan.*

Chapter 9: Magic in the Dark

1. Kahlil Gibran, *The Prophet*, p. 29.

2. Igor Filippov, "Memories from Moskow," *Meditation*, fall 1991.

3. Kahlil Gibran, *The Prophet*, pp. 80-81.

Chapter 10: Purpose

1. Patrick Harbula, "On Purpose," *Meditation*, fall 1989, p. 35. Printed with permission from Sandy Levey-Lunden. Sandy Levey-Lunden can be reached at www.sandylevey.com or by e-mail at OnPurpose@SandyLevey.com.

Chapter 11: You Are the Magic

1. Vivian King, *Being Here When I Need Me: An Inner Journey.* pp. 125-27. Printed with permission from Inner Way Productions.

Bibliography

Assagioli, R. (1965) *Psychosynthesis.* Penguin Books, New York.

Atkinson, B. (1968) "Nature." In *The Selected Writings of Ralph Waldo Emerson.* Random House, New York.

Barry, M. (1997) *The Awakening Princess.* Inner Way Productions, Findhorn, Scotland.

Borland, C. & Landrith, G. (1976) "Improved Quality of City Life through the Transcendental Meditation Program: Decreased crime rate." In *Scientific Research on the Transcendental Meditation Program: Collected Papers:* D.W. Orme-Johnson & J.T. Farrow, ed. (Vol. 1, pp. 639-648). Rheinweiler, W. Germany: Maharishi European Research University Press.

Capra, F. (1991) *The Tao of Physics.* Shabhala Publications, Boston, MA.

Castaneda, C. (1991) *Journey to Ixlan.* Simon & Schuster, New York.

Castaneda, C. (1992) *Tales of Power.* Simon & Schuster, New York.

Chopra, D. (2000) *How to Know God: The Soul's Journey into the Mystery of Mysteries.* Harmony Books, New York.

deLaszlo, V. S., ed. (1959) *The Basic Writings of C. G. Jung.* Random House, New York.

Foundation for Inner Peace. (1992) *A Course in Miracles.* Foundation for Inner Peace, Mill Valley, CA.

Gibran, K. (1977) *The Prophet.* Alfred A. Knopf, New York.

Jefferies, R. (1891) *The Story of My Heart.* Longmans, Green & Co.

Johnson, R. C. (1969) *The Imprisoned Splendor.* Hodder & Stoughton, Ltd., London.

Jones, W. T., ed. (1969) *The Classical Mind.* Harcourt, Brace & World, New York.

Keyes, K., Jr. (1982) *The Hundredth Monkey.* Vision Books, Coos Bay, OR.

King, V. (1998) *Being Here When I Need Me: An Inner Journey.* Inner Way, Findhorn, Scotland.

Niebuhr, U., ed. (1976) *Justice and Mercy.* HarperCollins, New York.

Payne and Bendit (1943) *The Psychic Sense.* Faber & Faber.

Tolle, E. (1999) *The Power of Now.* New World Library. Novato, CA.

Vancil, M., ed. (1998) *For the Love of the Game: My Story by Michael Jordan.* Crown Publishers, New York.

Various authors and issues. (1987–92) *Meditation.* Intergroup for Planetary Oneness, Granada Hills, CA.

Wilmherst, W. L. *Contemplations.* J. M. Watkins.

Zukav, G. (1990) *The Seat of the Soul.* Simon & Shuster, New York.

RECOMMENDED READING

Environment

Gore, A. (1992) *Earth in the Balance: Ecology and the Human Spirit.* Houghton Mifflin, New York.

Morgan, M. (1994) *Mutant Message.* HarperCollins, New York.

Quin, D. (1993) *Ishmael: An Adventure of the Mind and Spirit.* Bantam Books, New York.

Sheldrake, R. (1992) *Rebirth of Nature: The Greening of Science and God.* Bantum Books, New York.

Healing

Bailey, A. (1980) *Esoteric Healing.* Lucis Trust, New York.

Colgrove, M. (1991) *How to Survive the Loss of a Love.* Prelude Press, Santa Monica, CA.

Hay, L. (1999) *You Can Heal Your Life.* Hay House, Carlesbad, CA.

Siegel, B. (1986) *Love, Medicine & Miracles: Lessons Learned About Self-Healing from a Surgeon's Experience with Exceptional Patients.* Harper & Row, New York.

Psychology

Assagioli, R. (1973) *The Act of Will.* Penguin Press, New York.

Ferrucci, P. (1982) *What We May Be: Techniques for Psychological and Spiritual Growth through Psychosynthesis.* J. P. Tarcher, Los Angeles.

Janov, A. (1970) *Primal Scream.* Perigee Books, New York.

Jung, C. (1978) *Man and His Symbols.* Dell, New York.

King, V. (1998) *Soul Play: Turning Your Daily Dramas into Divine Comedies.* Ant Hill Press, Georgetown, MA.

Spirituality

Bach, M. (1961) *Had You Been Born in Another Faith.* Prentice Hall, Inglewood Cliffs, NJ.

Bach, R. (1979) *Illusions: The Adventures of a Reluctant Messiah.* Dell, New York.

Bailey, A. (1980) *Serving Humanity.* Lucis Trust, New York.

Barrett, W. (1956) *Zen Buddhism: Selected Writings of D. T. Suzuki.* Doubleday & Company, Garden City, NY.

Cahill, S. (1992) *The Ceremonial Circle: Practice, Ritual, and Renewal for Personal and Community Healing.* HarperCollins, New York.

Dial, J. (2001) *I Am the Beloved: Cosmic Wsidom from the Spiritual Source of Rev. Joy Dial.* Writers Club Press, Lincoln, NE.

Furguson, M. (1980) *The Aquarian Conspiracy: Personal and Social Transformation in the 1980s.* J. P. Tarcher, Los Angeles.

Mishlov, J. (1992) *Thinking Allowed: Conversations on the Leading Edge of Knowledge.* Council Oaks Press, Tulsa, OK.

Spangler, D. (1984) *Emergence: The Rebirth of the Sacred.* Dell, New York.

Yogananda, P. (1974) *Autobiography of a Yogi.* Self Realization Fellowship, Los Angeles.

Zimmerman, J. (1996) *The Way of Council.* Bramble Books, Ojai, CA.

Zukav, G. (2000) *Soul Stories.* Simon & Schuster, New York.

Index

About the Author

Patrick J. Harbula has been a spiritual teacher and life coach since 1985 when he was ordained by the Institute of Spiritual Awareness after completing a four-year ministerial program. He has reached hundreds of thousands with his empowering message of applying spirit-ual power and living life through the passion of soul purpose. Patrick continues to appear on radio and TV shows in the U.S. and Canada and is currently presenting lectures, workshops, and classes based on this book. He is the founder of the Living Purpose Institute and offers a Life Purpose Coaching Certification Program for those wanting to coach others to live their passion.

He also trained in psychosynthesis (a transpersonal psychology) under the late Dr. Vivian King from 1985 to 1988. In 1986, he found-ed *Meditation* magazine, a national, bimonthly publication, which presented a wide variety of meditative practice and emphasized the unity at the core of all philosophical and spiritual belief.

In 1993, Patrick advanced his career in publishing with Sage Publications, a world-renowned, social science publisher. As manag-er, and later, director, Patrick achieved unprecedented success for the company by applying spiritual principles to business strategy.

Patrick is also currently the president of the Spiritual Unity Movement (SUM), an organization dedicated to honoring the truths that are common to all spiritual understanding including light, love, compassion, truth, peace, and goodwill. For more information on SUM, you can visit **www.spiritualunitymovement.org.**

Patrick lives with his wife, Corina, and two stepchildren, Elizabeth and Alison, in Ventura County, California. He can be reached at **www.livingpurposeinstitute.com** or by email at **patrick@magicofthesoul.com**. For information on the Life Purpose Coaching Certification Program, classes, teleseminars, workshops, phone coaching, Primal Fire Retreats, board retreats, speaking, or corporate trainings, please visit the website or call **(866) 204-2261.**